"It would be a personal dream-come-true if every church leader and minister would read *Half Two* and use it to cast a new vision for their own congregation. I also hope that every church member over the age of fifty studies it in a small group setting and reflects upon its implications for their lives. Thanks, Wes and Judy, for writing such a powerful resource!"

Missy Buchanan
Writer/Speaker on Issues of Aging Faithfully
Author: *Spirit Boosters for the Journey of Aging*

"Many years ago as a young man in my thirties, my mentors—those who impacted and influenced my life—were much older, usually in *Half Two*. I learned quickly that the Lord had equipped them with talents, wisdom and spiritual gifts that played out the rest of their lives. They built legacies that continue to this day and for future generations. Wes has penned a book that needs to be read by the *over 50s* as it inspires us to continue, to be used for a purpose, and to impact lives. Equally important, **Half Two is a must read for the Millennial Generation**. It will give them great life perspective as they better understand *the whole, not just the part*. Thank you, Wes and Judy, for a powerful read."

Dave Burns, Director of Adult Ministries
Mount Hermon Christian Conference Center

"In his eloquent new book, Wes Wick calls on every one of us to make the best and highest use of all our experiences, for all our days. His examination of purpose, aging, and the church offers a powerful and purposeful blueprint for building stronger families and stronger communities everywhere. This book is heaven sent!"

Marc Freedman, Founder and CEO, Encore.org

"As a 35-year career military aviator, much of my career was spent in pre-flight planning, afterburner launches, mission execution and final landings—'each a journey and never a dull moment!' Thus, I was intrigued in joining Wes Wick's marvelous *Half Two* journey—one that challenges all believers to think seriously about what God is calling us to do with our remaining years. I commend this book to your reading—make sure to strap your seat belt on tight—you may never be the same!"

Major General Peter Sutton, United States Air Force (Retired)

"After twenty years of ministry, I've learned a lot from the *school of hard knocks*. How I wish *Half Two* had been available years ago. This resource is timely and appropriate as the Age Wave ushers millions into the Encore stage of life. Wes and Judy Wick's comprehension of the demographic is spot on. Every minister will benefit from reading this book. Not only is it insightful, it's humorous and original. It's easy to recommend to anyone over 50. Enjoy reading it. I did."

Peggy Fulghum, Adult 2 Ministries Associate
Johnson Ferry Baptist Church, Mariettta, Georgia

"As our population ages, there seems to be an either-or response—either a steadfast grasping at position and power, as if to stave off inevitability, or a rapid release, escaping into the comfort of a well-planned retirement stretching twenty-five or more years into the future. Meanwhile, many of the younger generation are looking for help—mentors who will empower them, experienced partners who will work with them, spiritual fathers and mothers who will teach them how to care for their souls.

"Wes Wick addresses these dueling concerns with an experienced, winsome, provocative, and passionate challenge, both to those approaching second half borderlands, and to the local church—which must be multi-generational or die. With deft humor and surgically precise questions for exploration, *Half Two* goes beyond analysis, providing strategic next-steps for engagement. Eminently readable, deeply personal, desperately needed, highly recommended."

Bill Dogterom, D.Min., Professor
Pastoral Ministries and Spiritual Formation
Chair (Religion) - Professional Studies, Vanguard University

"Engaging, inspiring, informative, funny ... all words I use to describe Wes' book. Such an easy and enjoyable read, with practical advice and straightforward implementation ideas— balanced with real life stories. You'll finish the book feeling motivated to make new friends with people close in proximity but not in age. Love *Half Two.* I encourage young and old to read this book."

Heather Crooker, Stay-at-Home Millennial Mom
Christian Berets Event Coordinator

"I found myself in tears after the introduction, and applauding for the encore at the end!

"Wes Wick writes with character, charm, a touch of humor— even the laugh-out-loud variety—and thoughtfulness. Though I fundamentally prefer not to group people by any defining mechanisms, i.e. age, gender, race, etc., this book addresses the natural inclinations to do so, and is loaded with insight and inspiration. Wes' passion for his calling models the practical guidelines and proffered wisdom shared throughout the book. He suggests that we not only think specifically, but also engage actively, in the wider, diverse realms of life at every age. YES! to *Half Two.*"

Nancy K. Christel, President and CEO, Sheeperfect®

"Wes Wick puts into words what I've been trying to communicate for years, while also offering fresh insight that I had not considered. As a pastor, I can confidently say that *Half Two* is a 'game changer' on how to integrate and value the beloved 'seniors' in my congregation. Wes is a first-class communicator, leaving the reader with not only head knowledge, but also with gut-wrenching emotions that will ignite your ministry vision.

Ryan Moore, Pastor, Christian Life Center, Santa Cruz, CA

"As someone who has fought vigorously for cross-cultural appreciation throughout my adult life, I deeply appreciate the cross-generational unity approach presented in *Half Two*. Laced with biblical insight and fresh examples throughout, Wes presents a Christ-honoring, church-unifying pathway that motivates us to make our second half years more fruitful."

Samuel M. Huddleston, D. Min.,
Assistant District Superintendent Assemblies of God,
Northern California and Nevada
Author, *Five Years to Life* and *Grand Slam*

"Wes & Judy Wick are leaders in the movement to challenge people to steward their second half of life well. Their ministry of YES brings the generations together to serve in helping others. Now, with the book *Half Two*, Wes captures their shared vision for living out your second half with hope and optimism that "the best is yet to come." Reading it will rock you out of your comfort zone and challenge you to live the rest of your life with purpose."

Richard & Leona Bergstrom, Co-Authors
Third Calling: What are you doing the rest of your life?

"As a college president, I work in a multi-generational environment observing constant interactions between young adults and 'other-than-young' adults. Wes Wick's outstanding new book, *Half Two*, is a delightful and compelling read not only for the over-50s, but for anyone seeking a better understanding of the unique and compelling ways God can use all of us in our lifespan's later years.

"As a believer, I've never thought God desires for us to push the hold button on our remaining years, and Wes' argument that we engage all the experiences of our lives to serve others is truly inspiring. With a rapidly growing aging population, the church has a terrific opportunity to leverage older believers to serve effectively in His kingdom work. Thank you, Wes, for a page-turner calling us to action throughout our lives!"

Jim J. Adams, Ed.D., President, Life Pacific College

"*Half Two* challenges us to take advantage of our golden years. Retirement does not mean *sitting on the sidelines*. Slowing down does not mean *stopping*."

Phil Oates, *BUZZ OATES*, Chair

"Wes Wick accomplishes what many authors fail to do — give clear solutions after detailing problems. Wes brings clarity to a critical American cultural issue. Speaking from experience, he equips readers with a remarkable, solution-oriented roadmap as they embark together on an incredible journey. Timely, relevant and tremendously needed in the life of every 'senior' — what you hold in your hand is not just a book — it's a gift. Read it and embrace it. Your life will never be the same!"

Chuck Stecker, Ph.D., President
A Chosen Generation and *The Center for InterGenerational Ministry*

"Anyone over fifty will benefit from reading this well-written, inspiring book! My wife Char and I started Assist International in our early fifties. Decades later, we know this was the best decision we ever made. I'm excited that *Half Two* will help others make similar life-changing, half-two decisions. Such excitement in following Christ full-throttle."

Bob Pagett, Founder, Assist International

"It's time that the church develop new strategies to better use the potential gifts of its 50-plus members. In most cases, they are untapped resources—just waiting to be recruited and empowered for service. *Half Two* goes a long way to provide inspiration and methodology for just that. Wes and Judy Wick have devoted themselves to bring this message to churches and individuals across the nation. This outstanding, *must-read* book is engaging and captivating."

Richard Dresselhaus, D.Min., Pastor, Author, Speaker

"Just say 'YES!' That's the best way to summarize our response while reading *Half Two*. Through insightful personal journey reflections, interactions with others, and Scripture, the book presents a compelling vision-to-action process. Whether you are a pastor or church leader (of any age), you WILL be challenged to create intentional pathways for unleashing boomers and older adults to engage in meaningful ways. And, if you are a boomer or older adult, reading this book will stimulate your thinking about significance and discerning God's call in Half Two."

Evelyn Johnson and **Alan Forsman**
Co-Authors, *Crescendo: An Ascent to Vital Living*

"If you are approaching or in retirement, know that God wants to *re-tire and re-fire* you for Kingdom-purposes. As you read this book, allow God to break old mindsets and re-shape your perspective on living out the next lap of life.

Reverend Dominic Yeo
General Superintendent, Assemblies of God of Singapore
Senior Pastor, Trinity Christian Centre

HALF TWO: The Quest for a God-Honoring Encore

Published by:
YES! Young Enough to Serve
www.yestoserve.org

Address all inquiries to:

Wes Wick
YES! Young Enough to Serve
1040 Creek Drive
Scotts Valley, CA 95066
Email: info@yestoserve.org

ISBN-13: 978-1977502100

Editor: Julia Young
Cover: Dan Pitts Design

Printed in the United States of America.
First Edition

HALF TWO

TWO

The Quest for a God-Honoring
ENCORE

Wes Wick

HALF TWO

The Quest for a God-Honoring Encore

ITINERARY

DEDICATION

IN MY MID-TWENTIES and newly engaged, I was driving from San Francisco to Southern California with my soon-to-be father-in-law Don Popineau and family friend Stewart Novarro.

We were returning from a weekend missions trip to San Francisco's inner city. I had sprawled out in the back seat, trying to catch up on sleep lost to blaring police sirens the night before. Don and Stewart were talking, and my sleepy ears awoke to their spirited conversation. Don, recently retired from his house-painting career, contemplated an invitation from the San Francisco pastor.

"Mel Johnson wants me to join his pastoral staff," Don confided. "And I'm seriously thinking about saying yes."

Unprepared for this kind of radical upheaval from an early fifties layman, retired and seemingly so firmly rooted in Southern California, I was astounded. In my mind, *older* adults don't leave the security of their suburban homes to minister in a rundown and drug-infested area of San Francisco. Certainly, I thought, he would come to his senses.

Or I would come to mine.

Don was a seasoned follower of Jesus who knew that his early retirement from a successful painting career was not a free pass to a self-absorbed life of leisure. Yes, he had a newfound sense of freedom, but he also fervently sought to live his life so that it counted for the kingdom.

Over the next months, he moved into a humble dormitory apartment, completed studies for his ministerial credentials, and began serving as a pastor at Glad Tidings Temple in San Francisco. After our June wedding in Southern California, my mother-in-law Peggy joined him. They rented out their Southern California home and leased a flat in San Francisco.

Over the next three and a half decades, I've had a front row seat to observe how spiritually fruitful life's second half can be as I have watched my father-in-law serve in San Francisco; plant a church in Southern California; complete numerous projects at a Christian college on the Central Coast of California; manage, upgrade, and re-sell apartment complexes; avidly read, study, and teach God's Word; offer poignant advice to ministers, friends, and family; and just plain "genuinely care for people."

Even at the time of this writing, at 89, 'Papa' Don makes twice weekly visits to Life Pacific, a Christian college two miles from his home, to encourage and pray with students at their chapel services—something he has done throughout his eighties.

Thank you, Don Popineau, for being a living epistle of Christ. I've had the privilege of knowing you only on your plus side of fifty. Your first half of life was also an incredible adventure, but thank you for showing so many others and me how fruitful *Half Two* can be. It's with great joy and honor that I dedicate this book to you, Papa Don.

I want to be like you when I grow up.

TOUR ORIENTATION

If you try to hang on to your life, you will lose it.
But if you give up your life for my sake
and for the sake of the Good News, you will save it.
Mark 8:35 (NLT)

YOU ARE CORDIALLY INVITED to take a close-to-home vision trip. On this quest, we'll explore the hills, valleys, plateaus, and undeveloped terrain of life's second half. We'll examine how American churches and ministries are responding to the exploding population of adults over fifty.

In our early to mid-sixties, my wife Judy and I have worked nationally for about ten years in second-half adult ministry. Though still relative newcomers to this season of life, we hope our perspective will grow with each passing year. So please be patient if I step on your toes or talk like a freshman tour guide with all the answers. We all have a lot more to learn and experience as this adventure unfolds.

We've divided this book into fourteen chapters or days. Easygoing readers may want to take a couple of weeks for this quest into the world of adults over fifty.

So, what is a *vision* trip?

Samaritan's Purse[1] recently invited Judy to experience her first vision trip, traveling with a team to Guyana in South America to witness firsthand Operation Christmas Child's gift distribution.[2] It greatly moved her to see these vibrant children opening their gifts and to sense the spiritual ripple effect of it throughout that region.

Although *missions trips* generate plenty of vision, a *vision trip* differs slightly in emphasis. It's often a shorter, experience-and-observation blitz designed for leaders—with the goal that participants return with an enthusiastic, infectious appreciation for the ministry—and a willingness to rally others.

That, too, is our goal for this two-week trek.

Perhaps some of you think missions and vision trips are out of reach physically or financially. But this *Half Two* vision quest is wide open to people of all ages, both leaders and followers. And we've done our best to make it physically accessible and financially affordable, traveling the USA on about a dollar a day.

And, of course, no passports, visas, shots, medical exams, waiver forms, support letters, strange-looking bugs, or unfamiliar foods that turn your stomach inside out—this time around. We'll save all that for a later trip.

Half Two?

Is this title the blunder of an ill-advised rookie author?

Of course, *'half two'* and *'have to'* add confusion and special twists from the get-go. Needing to spell both words of a book title in conversations is admittedly a bit cumbersome. But a lot of **have to** passion spills into these *Half Two* pages. We *have to* make changes in how we approach *Half Two*. We *have to* make it better! And we can.

We'll discuss how to do that on the pages ahead. We're honored to have you join us.

Is Your Best Ahead?

Conventional wisdom has it that our best is yet to come. Obviously with heaven in the equation, this is true. But what about our remaining days on earth? Is our best still ahead, or is our best behind us? While tomorrow holds no guarantees, I hope and believe **some** of my best days on earth are still ahead.

We see examples of people who proclaim life's second half to be better than the first—even for people like Job whose devastating midlife trials lead us to predict the opposite. But we also see examples of Christian lives that end with decades of misery and grief, never witnessing a Job-like turnaround. When God chooses to shower someone's second half of life with blessing, it's a gift to treasure and steward. It doesn't come through self-reliance or entitlement.

Much as in our marriage vows, we need to rely on the Holy Spirit so that we stay committed whatever comes our way: *for better or for worse, for richer, for poorer, in sickness and in health, to love and to cherish; from this day forward until death do us part.*

If life's second half holds the potential for some of our best days, months, and years, could a different, **better** path ahead lead us to what's best?

We sure think so and therefore invite you—before any of us expire—to new levels of perspiration, aspiration, and inspiration.

Do We Really *Have To?*

Some will question whether anything is really amiss in how we Christians approach Half Two in America. They hang on to the adage, "If it ain't broke, don't fix it."

Many trial-and-error social experiments with the 50+ population sadly leave us with more trials and more errors. Shortcomings stare us in the face. In our hearts, most of us know we can do better.

It's tempting to complain about these trials and errors but then pass the buck. We acknowledge potential for something better, but we often lack the individual and collective will to embrace the challenge. Perhaps we've fought our last good fight against the status quo and await someone with more energy, insight, and fortitude.

Meanwhile, energetic others choose to address more important issues. They may ask, "Why even attempt to change the paradigm for 'older adult' ministry? They don't necessarily want to change, and besides, they'll be gone soon."

It's similar to how we feel about some of our belongings—"old, broken, and not worth fixing."

We remember our kids testing the limits of our resolve. "*Do we **have to** clean up our mess, weed the flowerbed, get home by 10 pm...?*" Was ours an actual command, a strong suggestion, or just a mild one, with lots of wiggle room? Sometimes they'd break through our strict veneer; other times, we'd hold firm. And gradually, they learned to take personal responsibility and became more independent. We tried our best to avoid becoming helicopter parents.

Now working with folks at the other end of the age spectrum, we have no right to hover as we see adults entering another independent phase. We too, like late adolescents, are grateful to move beyond many of the earlier ***have to's*** of life. At this stage, older adults may simply say, "I don't *have to* volunteer at a food bank, host a small group, mentor teens. Been there, done that. I am retired!"

Pursuing Better

Many younger entrants into this second half of life, Baby Boomers and Generation X, seem financially ill prepared to sustain the retirement their parents enjoyed, much less make it better. Some are content to settle for the same or even slightly less, knowing they may earlier have blown through too much cash and have not saved as much.

Many others in Half Two perceive themselves to be living the good life. They've weathered the storm of raising teenagers; helped their kids through college; paid off their mortgage; placed their elderly parents in assisted living; said farewell to their boss and co-workers; walked away from nasty rush hour commutes; and just possibly started today with golf and walking the dog at the top of their agenda.

They've said goodbye to many *have to's* and are wary of adding new expectations. Many now feel entitled to settle into what they find pleasurable, comfortable, or entertaining. They've paid their dues, and this is their season to reap the rewards.

Some may react negatively to this sudden embrace of self-gratification, but let's not be too quick to rob others of newfound freedom's innate joy. Let's pause a moment, take a breath and celebrate their liberation with them. They may very well deserve to kick their feet up today or take a sabbatical for several months. *Free at last!*

But when they've rested and come up for air, we hope they, too, will join us in making Half Two better. I'm confident that stretching sabbaticals from four months to four decades is not God's idea of *better*. Obviously, we must coin a more astute definition of 'better'—hopefully charging ahead with stronger biblical understanding.

We appreciate John Coulombe—InterGen Pastor at EvFree in Fullerton, California—and his approach. When he hears individuals are retiring, he schedules an appointment with them six months beyond their career adieu. Prior to this appointment, he encourages them to golf, go on a cruise or two, sleep in, host a movie marathon, or to do other things they've put off until retirement. "Then come see me to talk about the rest of your life," he adds.

On many occasions, the retiree calls John, asking to make this appointment sooner. People get rested and restless more quickly than expected.

Encore!

On this two-week quest, we'll explore the untapped kingdom potential of Half Two adults. Most American churches we visit are not (yet) jumping to their feet, vigorously applauding and expecting more from the Encore Generation.

Encore Generation well describes adults over fifty. When we applaud them, we appreciate their earlier performance and hope to inspire more of their best going forward. They all were young once, and we have much to learn from their accumulated experiences and wisdom.

Young once myself, I was blessed to study in Vienna, Austria, in my early twenties. I enjoyed learning about the country's history, language, architecture, and classical music in morning classroom sessions. But to experience Viennese culture firsthand in grand buildings, parks, and along cobblestone streets—so much better.

Vienna has some interesting *encore* history and traditions. For example, each year the Vienna Philharmonic Orchestra still performs *The Radetzky March* and *The Blue Danube* as encores to their new year's concert. Adults in this enchanting city can be a bit starched and reserved, but I've seen them jump from their seats to enthusiastically encourage an encore.

Encore performances, often already planned, are not listed in the printed program. While we've come to expect them, they are meant to be a special treat, and the selection is often a surprise.

Ovations for encores differ from final applause. Audiences shouting *"Encore!"* so appreciate the preceding music that they ask for just a little bit more. Their preliminary ovation after the scheduled final number can affect the outcome of what follows. Perfunctory applause might truncate the production. Heartfelt, prolonged applause can impact the vitality and breadth of encore selections.

Does our Western culture need to elevate respect and encore appreciation for older adults? Absolutely, and well before any eulogies. While there's life, there's work for the kingdom — first act or encore.

In Titus 2 Paul admonishes older men and women to live lives **in the present** worthy of respect. Not a concluding ovation but a cheer for more — in the encore of life.

Pleasing God

Even if no one around us applauds, God eagerly awaits our encore performances post our main acts.

Following Scripture's lead, we can appreciate Half Two's freedoms even more when we find our pleasure in what pleases God.

In our final stretches of life, we can please God in many

ways. On this journey, we'll learn how to make Half Two *whole*, make it *His*, and make it *count*.

Though part of the Baby Boomer tribe, I don't intend to target only my generational cohort. Anyone over fifty is in our scope's crosshairs. And, as you'll see, we truly want younger generations to join us to inspire adults over fifty. When all generations appreciate the past performance of those older and eagerly anticipate their encores, it's a win-win.

Make It Whole points to avoiding partiality, self-sufficiency, or generational arrogance. This is a season to bring together the body of Christ as a unifying force, not disconnect ourselves from other generational members or proclaim superior insight. By humbly investing in other generations along this final stretch, we finish life well.

And, again, **anyone positioned to influence adults over fifty, please join us at the table, including those well under the fifty-year milestone.**

In Romans 12:3, Paul tells us not to think more highly of ourselves than we ought to think, but to use sound judgment, as God has allotted to each **a measure** of faith. We each bring a measure to the table as we further the kingdom in any way.

Christian readers may choose to skip over the *Make It His* section, assuming we're already doing that. But Half Two in America comes with subtle detours we need to avoid, including the pitfalls of self-centeredness and entitlement. When you get there, you'll know. We all need to avoid *the self-absorbed season of Me*.

Finally, we want to *Make It Count*. Let's look again at the

Great Commission, appreciate some inspiring Half Two stories, and watch Jesus' commands and commission purposefully at work in life's final chapters.

Let's be open to out-of-the-ordinary, God-pleasing encores, listening to God's voice, and embracing at the end of our journey — *"Well done, good and faithful servant."*

Half Two—
Make It WHOLE!

Onward,
FOREWORD to Destination I

Half Two—*Make It WHOLE!*

Dr. Ward Tanneberg

THE ARK OF THE COVENANT is a box made of acacia wood, according to God's own design, overlaid with purest gold; a reminder of God's blessing on Israel if the people obeyed him and his laws; a warning of despair, punishment and dispersion if they did not. The Ark made it through many tests and battles. Then one day, due to our disobedience and neglect, it was lost. It remains lost to this day.

There is, however, another "ark of the covenant," one created for the Church according to God's own design, overlaid with priceless tears. An intergenerational "ark" with a promise of blessing forever by its keeping. Now we are challenged to ponder; has the Church lost its "ark" again?

The psalmist utters a prayer for all 'Half Two' parents and grandparents—both biological and spiritual.

15

"Let me never be put to shame!"

He continues to reflect on blessings granted throughout his life journey. Then he reminds God of the intergenerational "ark."

> *O God, from my youth you have taught me,*
> *and I still proclaim your wondrous deeds.*
> *So even to old age and gray hairs,*
> *O God, do not forsake me,*
> *until I proclaim your might to another generation.*
> ~ Psalm 71:18 (ESV)

The psalmist is passionate in his cry to God. *All generations matter!*

In an era of duplicity and national crisis, Mordecai challenges his adopted daughter.

> *For if you keep silent at this time, relief and deliverance will rise for the Jews from another place, but you and your father's house will perish. And who knows whether you have not come to the kingdom for such a time as this?*
> ~ Esther 4:14 (ESV)

Mordecai is passionate in his cry to God. *All generations matter!*

No one said it would be easy, but Wes helps us get started.

Half Two—Make It WHOLE! is where author Wes unpacks the mess in which we find ourselves.

In Days 1 through 6, Wick sizes up the current state of 50+ *age wave* builders, boomers, and Xers. He stirs the glowing embers of older generations, extends a hand of hopefulness to the amazing generations who follow, and calls on us all to build bridges of faith and love, compassion and justice, reaching out intentionally to one another and to our world "for such a time as this."

Half Two—Make It WHOLE! is sobering and inspirational, purposeful and practical.

Wes is passionate in his cry to God. *All generations matter!*

Ward Tanneberg, Ph.D. Theology
Author, *Sacred Journey* and *Redeeming Grace*
www.wardtanneberg.com/blog/
Ministry Resources International

DESTINATION I. OVERVIEW

Half Two — *Make It WHOLE!*

He will restore the hearts of the fathers to their children
and the hearts of the children to their fathers,
so that I will not come and smite the land with a curse.
Malachi 4:6 (NASB)

IT'S HARD TO BELIEVE doctors used to make house calls. Today, it's at best a distant memory for most of us—or part of family folklore. But there's something winsome and wholesome about a general practitioner who knew family members and pets by name and who was versatile enough to treat a broad range of ailments.

We like to hang on to enchanted pictures of the past. Never mind the fact that women and children were dying in childbirth at alarming rates, and average life expectancy was under fifty. While some aspects of the past were truly wonderful, and often exaggerated, we tend to overlook some of their painful hardships.

In today's increasingly specialized world, we have a deep

and growing God-given yearning inside for **wholeness**. When some people hear the word 'whole', they think immediately of holistic medicine; the interplay between body, mind, and spirit; and the value of exercise and a good diet.

But in this book, we'll discuss wholeness in the context of disconnected body parts coming together. Particularly, we'll examine what happens when generations unite in more deliberate ways and go far beyond simple acknowledgment that other generations outside our camp exist.

At some earlier times, we've all been the exact age of everyone younger than we are now. Yet, we're sometimes prone to treat younger generations as aliens from other planets—and they often see us in a similar way. True, our life experiences at different points of history can undermine some common ground. But think of how much richer our lives can be when we tap into this variety of life experiences and viewpoints!

Removed from their God-designed intergenerational contexts, comparative terms lose their dancing partner. *Older* simply becomes *old and passé*; *elder* becomes *elderly, feeble, and forgotten.*

We live in the **United** States of America, and Judy and I serve as missionaries to this beloved nation. Unfortunately, though, we Americans often fail to live up to the unity embedded in the first word of our country's name. More than ever, churches need to show the *Divided States of America* what love and unity look like.

We are also founders of a Christian ministry and nonprofit

organization, **YES! *Young Enough to Serve***. *Young Enough to Serve* is not a declaration of independence—or a war cry proving to the world how capable some of us still are. It's a call to be faithful, humble conduits of God's love to current and future generations.

This is the path of wholeness we invite you to explore over the next several chapters—or days—as we crisscross together this enchanted land of Life Beyond Fifty. So, grab your suitcase, and let's finally get this trek rolling, first with an uphill ascent. Hopefully you weren't expecting only coasting on this coast-to-coast tour!

Day 1. TAKEOFF

Something's Not Right in California

He has shown you, O mortal, what is good.
And what does the LORD require of you?
To act justly and to love mercy
and to walk humbly with your God.
Micah 6:8 (NIV)

TEARS STREAMED DOWN Judy's face as she knelt beside her hotel bed and cried out to God. Earlier that day she had met separately with three older California couples, each from different churches, but all with similar stories of disappointment.

It was as though these three couples, who hadn't crossed paths, had rehearsed their stories beforehand. Their experiences were incredibly similar and sad. They each spoke to their feeling rejected in their churches because of their ages.

They spoke with Judy, a donor relations consultant for a Christian financial services company, who met with generous donors throughout the Western United States. These donors had already committed a portion of their estates to Christian ministries. They spoke animatedly about their families and were excited about the parachurch ministries and charities they were supporting.

All too frequently, though, conversations quickly spiraled downward as the subject turned to their home churches. "Here we go again," Judy thought to herself as she accepted a second cup of coffee. Listening to older adults gripe about their churches became a recurring theme. She did her best to redirect the conversation and to move briskly beyond the negative.

"I get the feeling that our pastor would be thrilled if everyone over sixty left our church. He treats us like we're standing in the way of progress," one gentleman confided.

His wife added, "They even insist that all the greeters at the front door are under thirty. For heaven's sake, even Walmart knows we can serve well in that role! We know how to be warm and welcoming to people of all ages."

Later that same day over lunch at a restaurant in a neighboring county, a well-dressed couple added their story.

"God has blessed us financially, and we give Him all the glory. We don't give generously with the expectation that we'll be given special honor or get our own way. Scripture teaches against that. But *goodnight*, being completely ignored and devalued is not what the Bible teaches either. In the secular world, nonprofits wouldn't survive if they treated donors the way we're treated in our church."

And the third couple later that afternoon helped complete the trilogy. "This church is where we raised our kids, served on the board, organized missions trips, led prayer meetings. We have no plans to leave, but it's terribly painful at this age to be in a church you've helped establish that has little regard for our past or our present contribution potential. We feel we still have so much to offer."

Judy encouraged these seasoned adults not to lose hope but to pray for understanding, and for their church leaders to understand and to change accordingly. Times were changing, however, and perhaps against these faithful sojourners; it was not easy for them to accept.

These were not shallow, unpleasant people; they were deeply committed Christ followers with rich histories and active prayer lives. They agonized at being put out to pasture—no longer valued. Caricatures of the *Church of the Past*, they felt no longer needed in the *Church of Today*. Some of these folks had quietly left sizable sums in their estate for their local churches, with a growing sense of givers' remorse.

While worship music was often part of these conversations, their angst went much deeper than decibels, drums, and genre. These older adults felt expendable, castaways in a throwaway culture. The first Boomers are now over 70; if the pattern continues, we younger Boomers might see our own demoralized faces in these snapshots in another decade or two.

Our trip is just beginning, and while filled with optimism, we've already noticed some turbulence in our ascent. And there is some rough terrain below.

Prone to Squander, Lord We Feel It

On this particular evening, Judy recognized something terribly wrong with the ways many American churches treated their older congregants, often forsaking the old to reach the young.

She cried out in frustration to God. "Your churches engage adults up to a certain age and then sequester them in a backroom Bible study. They'll throw in an occasional hymn sing, potluck, and field trip to appease them. Lord, you have not designed your Church to be exclusive. Please guide me, and let me know what You want me to do."

While Judy heard only one side of the story from her clients, it still became all too familiar and predictable. She sensed God calling her to do something, but she didn't yet know specifically what or where. She saw that others were shelving older adult potential, and sometimes these adults were burying their talents and shelving themselves.

At the same time, I served as Vice President for Advancement at a Christian university, charged with helping raise capital project funds. I also met often with generous, older Christian adults.

Establishing rapport, I asked, "Do you know of any

students from your home church ready to attend college or who are perhaps already attending our university?"

One responded, "No, there could be, but it's not something I'd be aware of. We really don't have much interaction with young people in our church. They do their thing, and we do ours. To be candid, at our church I don't think I know anyone under thirty by name."

How sad, I thought, that so many of these quality faith stalwarts had little or no interaction with younger people in their churches. What a tragic waste of experience, wisdom, time, and other resources. What a loss for the older adults as well, who might well enjoy surrounding themselves with vibrant young people. For me, working at a university with hundreds of young adults—who added much to my life—was sheer blessing.

To be fair, some older adults we know and churches we've experienced have reflected deep appreciation, love, and healthy expectation levels for all generations, but unfortunately, they have appeared to be in the minority— both inside and outside California, our home state.

Time to Dive In

Judy and I asked God to help move us from disheartened observers to active advocates for change. In summer 2007, Judy left her job and ramped up our initial efforts.

She has a background in children's ministry, and we have both served at Christian universities. We wanted to adopt an intergenerational approach that strove to unleash older adults' serving potential well beyond their peer group. We also wanted to bring younger generations along with us on this journey to help inspire us all.

We prayerfully considered names for this new ministry, and *YES! Young Enough to Serve* seemed a positive acronym. We prayed that God would use *YES!* to help build healthier bonds between generations, while challenging adults past Decade Five to keep their dreams alive.

Tale of Two Moms

"*YES!* just has to become a strong, national ministry!"

We heard this comment from an Arizona missionary couple who went on to share tales of their respective mothers.

When this couple moved to their overseas assignment several years ago, both of their moms were in their late sixties. One became a poster mom for what *YES! Young Enough to Serve* represents. The other, a polar opposite, literally pulled the shade on life and sank into deep depression.

As one mom approached age seventy, she ran for public office … and was elected! After serving two years with distinction, she shifted gears and wrote her first book. She saw the silver lining in her empty nest and retirement years — a chance to do more for others and go all out for God.

The other Christian mom settled first into complacency and then despondency. Fear got the best of her, and her last days became very dark and isolated.

While no church wants to see older adults dissolve into despair, this missionary couple perceived that many churches are passive about cultivating older adult serving potential and too accommodating of those settling for idleness.

The idle path may appear safer, but it's actually more treacherous. Although some underlying detail may be missing from these moms' stories, they highlight attitudes and choices that can prolong vibrant living or hasten death.

Discovering that you're still 'young enough' can add years to your life. Deciding prematurely that you're 'too old' may move your finish line closer.

We appreciate your joining us as we ask God to help us choose life—and invest in leaders who accentuate more fruitful later-life pathways.

After each chapter, we list probing questions that you can answer alone or in a group. Following is our first set:

- ✓ What are the costs of 'grin-and-bear-it' responses to ageism in the Church?
- ✓ What do you think is the healthiest way to respond? Why?
- ✓ All of us probably know Christians who finished life exceptionally well, and those who finished poorly. What were some keys to their success or premature decline?

Day 2. HARD LANDING

Throwing Grandma and Grandpa under the Church Bus

For everything there is a season, a time for every activity under heaven.
A time to be born and a time to die.
A time to plant and a time to harvest.
Ecclesiastes 3:1-2 (NLT)

IF WE COULD AGREE ON HOW American churches became so generationally divided, we'd be in a better position to move toward unity, right?

We live in a country intensely divided on a variety of issues. And some of that contentious spirit worms its way into our churches. While agreeing on origins of a problem may sound like a straightforward approach, conflict resolution comes with its own set of twists and turns. In the first place, we may not even agree that things are **not well** in the American Church. And assigning blame to contributing factors can stir up a hornet's nest.

We need renewed commitment to Biblical understanding

31

and divine wisdom!

In late 2007, Judy and I attended a conference in Southern California with pastors, second half church leaders, and laity from the United States, Canada, and other English-speaking countries, led by Ward Tanneberg, who has since become a dear friend and mentor. It was invigorating to know that we didn't stand alone in this ministry. Following this conference, Judy and I both sensed God's calling to pursue *YES!* full-time.

Houston, We Have Liftoff

YES! Young Enough to Serve took off in 2008, a year of national financial upheaval and the first year the oldest Baby Boomers (born in '46) could collect Social Security.

Our home church, Christian Life Center in Santa Cruz, California, graciously helped kick-start *YES!* With most basic expenses covered for six months, we assembled a team of prayer partners, established our founding board of directors, and filed official documents to become a nonprofit. Meanwhile, we met with multiple churches in Santa Cruz County to glean vision and mobilize adults.

We sensed enthusiasm in those early months, even while encountering occasional pockets of indifference, misunderstanding, or resistance.

The notion of church politics disturbs us. Worship wars. Conflict between generations. Self-interest. Galatians 5:15 (NIV) instructs, *If you bite and devour each other, watch out or you will be destroyed by each other.* Neither Judy nor I have much political savvy, but our passion is to see the Church rise up to be everything God intends.

Patronizing, Pacifying, and Pasture-izing

To capsulize concerns about this older adult untapped serving potential in the church, I wrote an article, "Throwing Grandma and Grandpa under the Church Bus." To my amazement *Christianity Today* featured it in its online publication, a welcomed blessing to us as founders of a new ministry and encouraging to me as a novice writer. I've included an excerpt here to give you a taste of its argument:

> In many families within your church, a very real and active faith in Christ has been passed down from generation to generation. Ask younger members of your church about persons of greatest spiritual influence, and chances are good that many will place a grandparent first on that list.

> To be fair, others from both inside and outside your church share in the impact, but grandkids will still often point to their grandparents as having the most significant impact on their spiritual journey.

SO, HOW'S THE BUS RIDE FOR THOSE IN YOUR CHURCH ON THE SECOND HALF OF THEIR TRIP?

How's church life for these graying sojourners who carry a biblical mandate to give testimony of God's power, wonder, and faithfulness to the next generations?

As you look at these saints who often have top-seed influence rankings in their families . . .

- Does your church family recognize and celebrate the current value of these elder travelers?
- Or do your older adults feel they're always being forced to take a back seat?
- How's your MPG, Miles Per Generation?
- Are you secretly praying for Tom Brokaw to personally adopt the group he hailed as the Greatest Generation?
- Are you convinced this traveling band of hymn-lovers is conspiring to throw your church into reverse gear?
- Have you thrown them off the bus or, heaven forbid, under the bus?

(The complete article is available online.[3])

Best-Laid Plans

In *"To a Mouse,"* Robert Burns contends, "The best-laid schemes of mice and men often go awry." Even with altruistic motives, our plans in both Christian nonprofits and churches can miss the mark.

HALF TWO — DAY TWO

We're still in flight. As we look out the window, we see multiple landing strips, and we're not exactly sure which one is the safest. The most popular landing site looks a bit tired and worn. It's time to find an alternate spot to land this jet.

One temptation Christian nonprofits face is seeing a need or opportunity the Church fails to address adequately and then with *tunnel vision* tenacity, creating a whole new system — apart from the church — to tackle it.

If we believe the local church is God's primary strategic method for reaching the world and making disciples, a chief emphasis of Christian nonprofits needs to gear toward strengthening local churches.

Do we act to make the local church stronger? Or do we give up on the local church and divert resources? Do we call people to remain faithful to their local bodies, or make them perhaps more cynical toward their local church? Do we bypass the Church in our efforts to do what we think is noble and right? Do we gloss over interdependent dynamics, blurring the picture of God's family, the Church?

We see parallel bypass dangers within churches, seemingly overlooking one generation to reach another. In some churches, age segregation takes over so completely that high school and younger students never rub shoulders with adults, apart from a handful of youth leaders.

When Sunday morning services are multi-generational, it's admittedly difficult to please God and everyone all at the same time. Churches with a more youthful bent may emphasize newer songs and the latest technology/ entertainment advances in sound, lighting, video, backdrop, and other atmospherics. Uniting generations can get lost in this mix, and older adults may feel out of place. If targets shift to older adults, worship leaders understandably fear they'll lose—and fail to attract—younger audiences.

We encourage adults to show lots of grace when it comes to worship. Getting to know the worship team members can help a lot. Regardless, sometimes a church service is like a bad haircut. Give it a week.

We love the heart of evangelist Luis Palau. Judy served on his Beachfest crusade team when he came to Santa Cruz, California, just after 9/11. When asked what he thought of the loud, high-energy music played at his crusades, he responded by saying, "I love the kids who love the music." May we strive for that same flexibility and compassion.

Some of us may be tempted to apply Palau's line in response to slower, more formal hymns. We, too, love the people who love the music.

But, when some older adults routinely delay their main sanctuary entrance until after worship, it may transcend unfamiliar lyrics, musical taste, tardiness, or stubbornness. Sometimes it's physiological. "The last time I tried to bravely endure worship, it triggered a severe migraine that lasted two days. The volume was much too high," one older gentleman shared as he greeted me in his church's foyer.

And a separate conversation at another church: "I used to think they were only gunning for my eardrums, but now my eyeballs are also under assault. Laser strobe lights troll the audience during worship. The blinding light gives me an instant headache and wreaks havoc with my friend's cataract surgery. She has to wear sunglasses during worship. Pretty weird, huh? Who would have thought worship could become dangerous to our health? What do we do? File an ADA complaint?"

Our current *generation-to-generation* faith transference faces more challenges than did our parents' transference to us. It's a profound test as huge numbers of Millennials walk away from their faith. Too often, though, we over-isolate the problem and settle for short-term fixes, cheap and expensive gimmicks, and workaround solutions—rather than uniting generations, strengthening families, and engaging seasoned veterans in this fight for the next generations' souls.

Involving older adults in outreach to those younger is not a circuitous path. Strategies that limit cross-generational engagement often set up the real detours.

Bounce houses, loud music and fog machines may seem like "no brainer" solutions to attract children and young people, but maybe our brains need to think more broadly and inclusively. What better solutions might also strengthen bonds between generations? Churches that routinely repel some generations to attract others inadvertently bypass God's generation-to-generation design.

If you are part of the Builder or Silent generation in a medium to large sized church, you have likely had silo structures in place for decades, attempting to minister separately and effectively to each age group. We've grown very accustomed to market segmentation.

Not long ago, I stepped curiously into an American Eagle outlet mall store. The ambiance and clothing line suggested a much younger demographic. Feeling out of place I quickly found the exit door, not wanting to look like a midlife male with an age identity crisis.

Inside our churches, signs on classroom doors may be less ambiguous than *American Eagle*, but we can still feel out of place. For example, Boomers and older Gen Xers walking into a "50+" ministry may immediately encounter reverse magnetic fields. They are reluctant to even dip their toes in this Half$_2$Ocean's H$_2$O—feeling much too young for this salty group and fearing 'wilt by association'.

In our inaugural years of *YES!*, we boldly defended older adults as Church victims of ageism. One pastor introduced us as *union stewards for older adults*. We don't want to discount the reality of ageism and its injustice; indeed, we seek to correct it for ourselves, for others in our peer group, and for those older than we.

But, we also know we are not the only ones feeling out of place.

✓ How do you describe your church climate between younger and older generations? Warm and sunny? A bit cold and apathetic? Some turbulent winds of discord? Cloudy with a potential for rain?

✓ Or perhaps there is no "between" to describe since either the older or younger fail to emerge in your climate zone. Are you ready for climate change?

✓ In our fast-paced culture of planned obsolescence, what is the proper role of older servers in your church?

Day 3. GROUND RULES

Accepting Our Share of the Blame

*I looked for someone among them who would build up the wall
and stand before me in the gap on behalf of the land
so I would not have to destroy it, but I found no one.*
Ezekiel 22:30 (NIV)

SUGGESTING WE WHO ARE OLDER AND WISER
may share blame doesn't sit well with lots of folks. We have
things figured out, and by golly, we're the victims here.
Generational gaps result from external factors over which we
have no control, right?

Some of us older ones may say, "Those kids are so tethered
to their technology. They won't even look adults in the eye."

"Millennials aren't committed to church life like we were.
Working couples have a lot on their plate and a wide screen
TV beckoning at home. Some manage to fit church into the
margins, but that's primarily to connect with their peers.
We're completely off their radar."

Life experience should help produce wisdom, but some life
lessons die on the vine when we always assume the role of the

overly ripe, overlooked, and discarded fruit.

We've seen this victim mentality take root in old, cantankerous curmudgeons and in some younger killjoys as well.

Peppering the Sulk Shaker

The eye cannot say to the hand, 'I don't need you!' And the head cannot say to the feet, 'I don't need you!' 1 Corinthians 12:21 (NIV)

In this verse, it's common to correlate older adults with the forsaken foot and hand. And we assertively follow up with, "Don't let anybody tell you you're no longer needed!" But the targets in this verse for changed behavior are the head and the eye. Let's break from our victim role and adopt the vantage point of the head and the eye, in need of a tweak. To whom do we say, "I have no need of you"?

As we began working with multiple churches, we quickly saw a pattern. Second half adult ministry has too often become a closed generational circle, with older adults caring for older adults. Leaders and assistants are commonly over age fifty. Adults under fifty in this area of specialized ministry are anomalies.

Other settings with older adults tend to outpace churches in their engagement and employment of young people. It's common to see late adolescents and young adults serving older adults in active retirement and assisted living communities, nursing homes, home health care, hospitals, and other treatment facilities—in both paid and volunteer positions.

There are some rare and invigorating church leadership exceptions such as Dr. Amy Hanson[4], well under fifty, who has embraced leading roles in 50+ ministry since her early twenties. At 23, Amy became the full-time active adult minister at Central Christian Church in Las Vegas, Nevada, where she led a 50+ ministry of over three hundred adults for five years.

Amy's enthusiasm, two decades of experience, and extensive related education invigorate us. We salute the Las Vegas pastor who saw her passion and poise—and took a risk (not a gamble). But that exceptional hire occurred about twenty years ago. Even with Amy's glowing success in this field, we still rarely see adults under fifty leading 50+ church ministries.

The more common peer-to-peer paradigm may seem healthy, considering that in some churches *nobody* reaches out to adults over fifty. It seems to flow naturally in our age-segmented culture, and we understand common objections coming from those older:

- Young people have not yet experienced life over fifty.
- We're on completely different pages. Can the Church realistically prepare young people to lead us older parishioners?
- Why should younger adults care?
- What would you expect? Did we really care about 'older adults' when we were much younger?

Only Peers Appearing

Please don't think we're suggesting something is inherently wrong with **peer-to-peer ministry. It has tremendous value. But as a stand-alone, it is also incomplete—like a half-baked pie or half-written book**. And it limits the depth and scope of our making disciples. In a later chapter, we will examine ways in which peer-only relationships can also be insufficient in nurturing faith in younger people.

Too often, everyday challenges remind us that we all need one another. For instance, it has become comically predictable to see half a dozen over-fifty adults huddled around a computer and projector at second half adult leadership conferences, trying to correct mysterious technical glitches. Sad to admit, but younger adults, even teenagers, could solve these tech problems in a millisecond with their eyes closed.

A key takeaway from 1 Corinthians 12 is that the Church is an *interdependent* body. The **whole** body needs to show concern for each **part**. And each **part** needs to concern itself with the **whole**. There are many applications here. In our context, it's particularly poignant as we consider how generations relate to one another.

At a typical youth conference, the names of young leaders from the Bible—David, Joseph, Daniel, Timothy, Mary, mother of Jesus—take center stage, reinforcing the significant role young people can play in the life of the Church. Similarly, as older adults congregate, names of significant, older biblical leaders emerge—Moses, Joshua, Aaron, Anna, Simeon—giving hope to aging men and women who might otherwise be tempted to throw in the towel.

Relating to each age group in a personally inspiring way makes sense. **But are we missing important reminders to value leaders at the opposite end of the age spectrum?** Young lives need to matter to those older, and older lives need to matter to those younger. We get into trouble when we trumpet the potential of only our peers.

Poking through well insulated social circles of adults over fifty, let's acknowledge not just how much younger people need us but also **how much we need them and how we even need to become like them.**

HALF TWO — DAY THREE

So, although our destination on this vision trip is to the Land of Life Beyond Fifty, we discovered today that we're not visiting an island. This is not a culture best experienced in isolation. Most of our heroes are found among those deliberately connecting to other generations, not just their own.

When the disciples circled the wagons to keep children at bay, Jesus rebuked them. He took children into His lap and blessed them. He highlighted how much His inner circle of adult disciples needed to become like these little children. At that moment, He wasn't talking about how much the kids needed them. That was a given. **We need to acknowledge** how lost we are without them—and how much we need to learn from them, from their trust, innocence, transparency, and free acceptance.

And, as Ted Cunningham[5] points out, "It's hard to mobilize a generation when you spend your days rolling your eyes at them."

The Foibles of FUBU

In 1992 <u>f</u>our <u>u</u>rban <u>b</u>rothers <u>u</u>nited to form the American clothing company, *FUBU*, an acronym that later came to be known as *For Us, By Us*. While effective in selling hip hop apparel, *For Us, By Us* is a lousy slogan and strategy for any church generational groups; however, in practice, many have become just that.

In that same 90's decade, Judy and I almost succumbed to a closed-circle paradigm as we contemplated naming our church's children's ministry outreach, *Kids Reaching Kids*. But with more thought, we realized that name drew a limiting circle around those great kids' potential. Instead, they needed to know they could reach out to others beyond the circle, that God could use them to touch older generations, too, including those of their older siblings, parents, grandparents, and great-grandparents.

We adopted the more open-ended *KidReach* name and were blessed to see children actively ministering both within and beyond their peer group.

One Sunday our pastor gave an altar call, and eyes were

glued to his six-year-old son Peter who walked forward. We expected him to kneel with others at the altar, but Peter had other plans. He laid his hand on the shoulder of an older man already kneeling. At his tender age, he prayed from his heart for this gentleman, a special moment that touched all who witnessed it.

Having served in Christian college administration for a couple of decades, I've sat through numerous graduation speeches, most very inspiring and some painfully laborious.

A few years ago, we attended a university graduation ceremony for two family members, and three separate speakers referred to the positive impact this graduating class would have on *their generation*. These vibrant speakers likely meant it more broadly than only their generational peer group, but it sounded like a young adult *FUBU* version of *kids reaching kids*.

I wanted to shout out to these students that with God's help, they have the potential to affect **every** living generation and future generations, not only their peers. (Judy was grateful I remained silent.)

Mind the Gap

Introduced in the late 60s in the London Underground, *"mind the gap"* called attention to the space between the station platforms and subway train doors. London and the current UK still use this visual and auditory warning. Unfortunately, the American Church has no such warning system in place that calls attention to widening generational gaps.

The Church often fails to acknowledge that we who are older need younger people in our lives, and vice versa. **We've been careless in minding the gap. Where do we go from here?**

- **Confession**: It's good for the soul, and it's good to help get the soles of our feet moving in the right direction. If we've allowed those outside our peer group to become peripheral or non-essential, let's confess this sin of omission to God. Ask for His help in leading us to younger and older friends who might help pop our peer-only bubbles. Then, let's confess to others how much we need other generations in our lives. (This is a common confession of older adults in care facilities, but most of us are in a better position now to act on our confession. The longer we put it off, the more difficult this problem, and acting on it, becomes.)

- **Inclusion**: Just as older adults don't appreciate the *Church of the Past* moniker, understand that younger Christians don't just represent the *Church of the Future*. They, and we who are much older, are part of *Today's Church*. Jesus said, "You *are*" — not *will be* or *were* — "the light of the world." In Christ, we all have present-tense potential to shine in the darkness.

- **Intentionality**: If we're an uncle, aunt, grandparent or possibly a great-something, we've got a good head start. Let's add some spiritual emphasis to these roles, and open the door to more conversations, asking good open-ended questions. Let's pray consistently and fervently, and let them know they are in our prayers.

- **Help**: Let's ask for help occasionally—but not like the grandparents in the Ally Bank commercial whose desperate tech needs seem to overshadow their love for their grandkids. (Dispensing with front-porch hugs and kisses, they immediately introduce their arriving grandkids to a plethora of tech devices they can't figure out.[6]) And, remember to reward them appropriately.

- **Expand Our Friend Base**: Let's become friends with our kids' and grandkids' friends. Moving beyond referring to them only as friends of our offspring, let's adopt them directly as our friends, too. If they show up in your home, call them by name for starters. Ask some good open-ended questions about them and their families. Share stories. Laugh together. Without crowding time with their peers, carve out some quality time, even if you need to use food as your passport. Don't just set it out; serve them and use that time for more quality conversations. If you're prone to forget details, jot down notes while your memory is fresh. As friendships progress, they may even friend you on Facebook. Accept this social friendship, too, and keep in touch with them through it.

- **Their Interests**: Let's re-align some of our interests to correlate with interests of younger generations. Be open to learn and appreciate new music—or learn more about rugby, rock-climbing, lacrosse, or figure skating, sports and activities we may not have participated in as children. It's not all about their tracking with our interests. Let's take the time to appreciate and engage in their world—and learn from them.

- **Our Interests**: If we're avid *or even average* golfers, fishermen, woodworkers, writers, musicians, chefs, seamstresses, etc., let's offer our skills to our children and their youth leader(s), and together with their parents and grandparents, let's find ways to engage young apprentices. One of our younger *YES!* board members treks about with her grandpa on Saturdays to bid on vacated storage units. *Who knew?*

- **Food**: It's a universal language in which young people are fluent. Bake cookies or a pie for the youth group. Treat them to a burger, fries, and a shake, or a homemade pizza.

- **Teach/Volunteer**: Let's not assume our days of teaching, leading, or helping out in the youth group or after-school programs are over. Teachers can mentor in writing, math, studying for exams, and more. If you have expertise in building, business, or piano playing, you have knowledge to share.

- **Support**: If we're able, let's support young people as they raise funds for a missions' trip or a school project.

- **Go International**: If you live near a university, check out International Students, Inc.[7], a Christian ministry that helps you establish friendships with international students or visiting scholars.

- **Go Intergenerational**: Sign up for a church small group of mixed aged, mixed ethnicity members. Or start one of your own.
- **Engage Young Leaders**: Ask your pastor or leaders of generationally focused ministries to read the day-five chapter, which recommends that such teams build more natural bridges between generations.

Every generation is worthy of our time investment, and we all benefit when we mind age gaps—from both directions.

✓ What, if anything, on the above list sparks your attention?

✓ Will you commit to praying about it?

✓ And then, as God directs, will you act? How soon — today, this week, this month?

✓ Perhaps you're ready to dive right in immediately, or maybe you need to take a preliminary step that helps unlock one of these doors. Or God may prompt you to share some other new direction ahead. What step(s) could you take with God's direction?

Day 4. SCHEDULE

So, When Does Half Two Begin?

*So the LORD blessed Job in the second half of his life
even more than in the beginning.*
Job 42:12a (NLT)

DO YOU REMEMBER WHEN SOMEONE FIRST OFFERED YOU a senior discount without your asking for it?

In my mid-fifties, I encountered this unexpected jolt. While I was not ready for the *senior* label, I was cheap enough to accept the discount. There, unsolicited, on my receipt was a 'senior soda'.

When I later learned their senior discount started at age sixty, I was ready to trade my Sprite for a bottle of Grecian Formula. But for those of you still south of sixty reading this paragraph, get ready. Your senior Sprite will be fizzing before you know it.

Don't get me wrong. I appreciate the thought behind the discount and the discount itself, but I wasn't yet ready to join this fraternity.

Just prior to Judy's fiftieth birthday, she received … and then ran … her first AARP invitation to the recycle bin. Aging brings some measure of grief, and the first step in the grief cycle is **denial**. *No, not us and certainly not now!*

And as a cautionary word to other men who, like me, are a bit younger than your wife … never call her over to the register to use her senior discount. Not a good idea. Just trust me on that.

As juniors in high school and college, we eagerly anticipated our upcoming segue to **senior** standing. Now 'senior' summons images of Cub Scouts carefully ushering us across the street. For many, senior class pride evaporated decades ago.

What's in a Name?

How do we generically define adults over fifty? *Primetimers, seniors, young at heart, sages, silver saints, forerunners, mature, or seasoned adults?* Fifty-plus is probably the most direct way to express it, but it's a bit too numeric. Briefly, we could use *Boomer* to identify adults in the earlier stages of the fifty-plus adventure, but that was short-lived. Generation X invaded "the fifties" even as early as 2015.

It's no wonder then that we like the term 'Encore Generation' to describe adults over fifty. It's a healthy image of someone still willing and eager to perform the encore whose dynamics differ from those in the earlier numbers. We tap into our range of giftedness—athletics, business, writing, medicine—and pull out our very best chords for our final anthems. These may resemble others of our songs, or they may sound completely different. But in them, we devote the best of our remaining energy to finish well.

Some *Encore Generation* adults choose to move in new directions and lay their more obvious career skills aside. They bring to the forefront latent interests, aptitudes, and abilities somewhat buried in the background for decades. Renowned American folk artist Grandma Moses, for example, began painting in earnest at the age of 78.[8]

YES! Young Enough to Serve defines our target group as *adults over fifty*, and we use *life's second half* in our tagline. Thank you, Bob Buford, for writing the book *Halftime*[9] that pushed many of us to contemplate the pivot to life's second half.

When does this mysterious second half of life actually begin?

Some argue that fifty is much too early to define as the start of life's second half. Perhaps we will live past one hundred; perhaps we will get struck down by lightening at 55; perhaps … but there's too much conjecture here. Women tend to live longer than men, but there's no promise.

Life expectancy tables show us that most of us begin our second half **well before fifty**. In fact, the average American male hits this threshold **before he is forty**, and on average, women reach it **shortly after forty**.

Still in Your First Half? Not So Fast

I recently said goodbye to my dear brother Ron, 79, just beyond the average American male's life expectancy. Good with numbers, he'd never have guessed his second half of life would begin at 39 one day in October 1976. Although he struggled with dementia in his seventies, I still appreciate how vibrantly he lived most of the years beyond his 1976 halfway mark. And even with his short-term memory loss, he brought others joy to the very end.

In earlier life stages, it's easier to tie events to specific ages. Kindergarten starts at age five, driving at sixteen, and voting at eighteen. Thirty seems old, fifty is the new thirty, yet people may collect Social Security at sixty-two and start Medicare at sixty-five. You **may** retire in your sixties, earlier, later, or not at all. If you have children, the empty nest may occur as early as your late thirties, at repeated intervals, or never at all.

If you're thirty-eight, did you know that half of America is now younger than you?[10]

Surprisingly, the average age for first-time grandparents is forty-seven. For Judy and me, that blessing waited until after we were sixty.

To say at age sixty-three that I'm still in my first half of life is optimism run amuck. For persons under forty to assert they are in their first half may be realistic, but it's also presumptuous.

Because we don't escape the womb stamped with an

expiration date, we can't assume everyone in their teens, twenties, or thirties is still in life's first half. Steve Jobs unknowingly moved into his second half of life at 28, dying at 56. We all know people who departed from this life much earlier than we may have expected.

Princess Diana reached her halfway mark at 18, Elvis Presley at 21, JFK at 23, Whitney Houston at 24, and Michael Jackson at 25.

While numbers are non-specific, by our mid-fifties, we have entered life's Half Two before eternity with Christ. Some of you fully accept that you're in life's final quarter. Some enjoy declaring that you're in 'overtime', beating the odds and living on borrowed time.

A few years ago, my father-in-law sought estimates for a new roof. One estimator gave him price options for either a 25 or a 30-year roof. He countered with, "How 'bout a five-year roof?"

Aha!

Okay, we know how life's second half ends, and enough speculating about when it begins. Why is the transition to Half Two significant?

When we acknowledge that years in the rearview mirror exceed those in front of us, it can become a sobering aha moment. For some, this thought contributes to a midlife crisis, turning life as usual on its head, sensing that it's *now or never* to live out some earlier wild fantasies. This *now or never* recognition can also create a sense of urgency that leads to more responsible, positive action—what Buford dubs *"moving from success to significance."* And, of course, God calls under-achievers to lives of significance, too.

This second half realization can also trigger reflection on the reality of our own mortality and the hope of heaven.

A friend in his early fifties shared with me that he wasn't yet ready for the 50+ ministry of *YES!* because he was still in *"a busy, upwardly mobile time of life."* He is very engaged in his career, with teenagers still at home, and he hasn't yet crossed a line when he might be tempted to coast downhill. While the life of a 70-year-old retiree can be hugely different from that of a 52-year-old bank executive, it's still not too early for churches to help influence thinking about the new road ahead.

The 70-year-old has some life perspective that could help our 52-year-old friend, and certainly vice versa. Even if the 52-year-old isn't ready to identify with the 50+ group, he would benefit from occasional lunch appointments with older mentors.

Half Two is not an old dusty road to avoid or postpone; it's a new avenue that deserves thoughtful reflection and preparation of the heart. Some of that preparation comes through quality time with more experienced trailblazers.

Interestingly, this friend thought *YES! Young Enough to Serve* should have a later starting point, after we reach an apex in life. Who's to say we don't keep moving upward and onward in our life experiences, wisdom, spiritual passion, and influence? Yes, aging can present huge physical challenges and temptations to withdraw from action—all the more reason to approach this season with godly ammunition.

Another adult, much younger, wanted to equate our focus on life's second half with hospice care, but so much life happens in our second half years—well outside the tender care of hospice.

Many churches select a later starting point (e.g. 55, 60, 65) for specialized ministries related to second half adult ministry. Whatever age you pick, know that you'll find adults beyond your starting point who think they're too young. We meet people all the time who perceive they're still too young to be 'young enough'.

Several summers ago, friends called us from a restaurant on the East Coast. They had stopped for lunch in a town saturated with older adults. They laughed out loud, noticing that the senior discount started at **age 85**. Pretty much everyone in that New England hamlet would have qualified for a senior discount if the restaurant had adopted a more typical starting point.

In her early days of teaching at Stanford, Dr. Laura Carstensen, director of the Stanford Center on Longevity[11], saw many empty seats in her *Adulthood and Aging* undergraduate classrooms. When she later changed the class title to reflect the study of longevity, her classes filled up quickly and had long waiting lists. She recognized that college students have a keen, personal interest in living long lives, but they are less motivated to study the current aging population and the dynamics of aging.

Yes to longevity; no to aging. Like many of us, these students want to live long lives without growing old in the process.

HALF TWO — DAY FOUR

We're learning that this Encore Generation has some inhabitants who are slow to accept their citizenship. They're not so sure they want to be treated as natives in this Land. And many seem ready to permanently disavow any relationship to this country, committed to being forever young.

They think they can beat the system. A whole lot of optimism ... and denial!

Twenty Steps Ahead

In our forties, Judy and I got excited about a dining room addition for our home with some tall windows to help capture the outdoor beauty of our environment in the Santa Cruz Mountains, surrounded by towering redwood trees. We drew up some initial sketches and then met with Dick Mulliner, an architect who was about two decades older than we and who volunteered at the university where I worked.

After looking at our sketches, he politely set them aside and said, "I'd love to help you with this project, but let me first ask you a question. Of your four kids, how many are still living at home?"

At that time, our twins were heading off to college, and we still had two sons at home.

"Much more quickly than you now realize, your four kids will be out of your home. You will find yourself caring for a much bigger house than you need, along with the additional weight of a second mortgage or home equity loan. As much as I'd appreciate your business, if I were in your shoes, I wouldn't go through with this project."

Until that conversation, we were caught up in the moment, excited about this new creative adventure. We could easily tie our dream to God-honoring motives such as hospitality and becoming better stewards of the view of His beautiful creation. But Dick's elder voice of wisdom was timely and invaluable. In fact, had we not heeded it, we may not have been in position to later take the leap of faith to start YES! And, for sure, we'd have more windows to wash.

Our forties and fifties are great times to take short-term missions trips, as schedules allow, investigating possible future serving endeavors. And it's also an opportune time to coach and mentor those younger.

How one exercises such freedoms as the empty nest or paying off a mortgage can be precursors to what's ahead. Freedom is often doled out incrementally. Be faithful in the little, and God will show Himself faithful as freedoms grow.

Voices and Choices

Let's be clear. Thought patterns related to Half Two take

shape early. Secular media will not hit the pause button, patiently waiting until we reach a certain magical age in our mid-sixties or later. The Church must lead in this battle for hearts and minds, reinforcing Christ-honoring, unselfish attitudes toward new Half Two opportunities/ challenges—like the empty nest, grandparenting, caring for aging parents, parenting adult children, retirement, and passing our faith on to younger and future generations.

We've noticed a few healthy shifts in secular advertising, now occasionally moving beyond predictable retirement stereotypes. For decades, retirement commercials have featured a healthy, older married couple hand-in-hand, in or near soothing water such as a beach scene, swimming pool, or hot tub. Fortunately, some advertisers now help debunk the myth that retirement years primarily know vibrant health, blissful abandonment, and endless leisure.

Hand in hand into the forever? But, of course, many on this journey have always been single or are *single again* through death or divorce.

Financial preparation for life's later years deserves careful attention, hopefully with spiritually sensitive advisors who know there is more to life than amassing personal wealth. Thoughtful preparation helps us build a healthy foundation for the years ahead when we may not be drawing a salary. It can also add exciting, practical breadth to our generosity and range of Half Two possibilities.

But many of our second half ministry colleagues agree that our American financial planning culture places disproportionate emphasis on retirement as the future savings centerpiece—almost to the exclusion of applying godly wisdom and discernment to our decision to retire vocationally, postpone retirement, or launch an encore career.

Are we really willing to let God fully direct this new stage of life? Or, are we predefining for ourselves the parameters within which He can work?

The foregone conclusion of retirement bothers me in much the same way some presume every single person is destined for marriage. Death and taxes—not marriage and retirement—made it to Benjamin Franklin's short list of life's certainties.[12]

We're tempted to follow in lockstep with our culture. We often fail to pray for divine guidance in life's later years, except when encountering illness, estrangement, or other unexpected hardship. It has become a DIY adventure, too often with a 'laissez-faire' attitude toward God.

Our friends, Richard and Leona Bergstrom, recently authored a powerful book, *Third Calling*[13], related to this stage of life. They are passionate about helping Baby Boomers move into this season with greater determination to listen to God's voice, allowing Him to give shape to our 'third calling'. They ask, "What are you doing the rest of your life?" They have also been very helpful to me as I have written this book, my first—which, incidentally, is part of my answer to their book's important question.

✓ Are you ready to help others discover a more fruitful path for life's second half? You may not want to publicly share their names, but who might you help nudge forward? Perhaps simply ask them to join you in an upcoming serving event. What other actions might you consider?

✓ Who are younger people you could ask to pray for you?

✓ Who are some mature adults a bit farther down this path who can help you avoid some potential pitfalls lurking ahead?

Day 5. HONORING FELLOW TRAVELERS

Making Room for Young Leaders

Even when I am old and gray, do not forsake me, my God,
till I declare your power to the next generation,
your mighty acts to all who are to come.
Psalm 71:18 (NIV)

ONE OF THE HALLMARKS OF *YES! YOUNG ENOUGH TO SERVE* has been our generationally diverse board, usually spanning five or six decades, from the Twenty-Somethings to Seventy-Somethings. We are all still learning our way toward spreading our message, but inviting young leaders to partner with us in this adventure has been invaluable.

We're certainly not the first intergenerational advocates who push for renewed commitment to bridge generational division. Many have a vision for deepening relationships outside their peer group. And many churches have made deliberate moves in this direction.

As each of us personally seeks opportunities to declare God's power to the next generation, we long to see this cross-generational concern embedded more deeply and deliberately in American culture, including, but not limited to, our American church culture.

Any Schisms in Your Scope?

Too often, we hear complaints about generational gaps that avoid personal responsibility and seem to go nowhere. Leaders count nickels and noses in separate age-targeted programs, but we commonly fail to measure growing chasms *between* age groups.

Your church may have a strong multi-generational mix, with eight or nine decades of life well represented. Or, you may live in a community where a younger or older demographic dominates, and your church may accordingly reflect a narrower age swath.

Church size also has a noticeable impact on how closely our generations connect with one another. Experience has shown us that generational separation is more pronounced in larger churches—most noticeably when there has been no consistent, intentional effort to unite the generations.

Gaps don't necessarily convey contentious relationships. More commonly, they are relationships characterized by indifference—out of sight and out of mind. We take it steps farther by becoming indifferent to our own indifference.

The generational *silo* approach has been the heart and soul of many, but not all, larger churches throughout the last half-century. It carries with it the built-in belief system that tends to value specialization over integration, allowing generational gaps to get wider over time.

Even as a young teen I wondered how my home church could attach the 'Family Night' label to our midweek gatherings. For our family, it meant a quick waffle dinner and then off to church, each going into our specialized, age-segregated silos before finally reuniting with my parents and siblings for the sleepy ride home. And, of course, the next morning we darted off to our age-segregated schools.

While we individually benefited from specialized programs for each member of our family, those Wednesday nights separated our nuclear family and the broader church family as well. It pulled our families apart, not together.

Please know that these evenings were fun, spiritually nurturing, and instructive—for the most part. Looking back, I just smirk at our calling it 'Family Night'.

Shifting Gears

Generational gaps do not respect church size, and a small church size does not guarantee a close-knit family with strong intergenerational appreciation and relationships. Many small churches are mono- or bi-generational, leaning younger or older. To become more intergenerational, they may need to think beyond the scope of their current congregation.

For example, if your church is predominantly older, consider meeting with the elementary school principal nearest your church. Ask the open-ended question, "How might our church bless your school?"

Depending on the principal's faith background, there may be some hesitation and suspicion, but he/she will typically appreciate being asked. The answer may be a material need such as a new flag or start-up paper supplies for each class. Conversations might also lead into needs requiring volunteer time such as afterschool tutoring, teacher aides, free car washes for the school staff, or a campus cleanup day.

Will hordes of students start pouring into your church as a result of these efforts? Probably not. But it represents a turn of the heart toward children and an intentionality the Lord will reward. You want the older to start thinking about and caring for the younger, and vice versa.

While some of us vocally advocate for stronger relationships beyond our peer group, we cannot assume other church members and leaders share this same burden or passion. Ironically, we wouldn't settle for cross-generational indifference and distance within our own families, but it's sometimes a different matter within our church families.

The sometimes-bumpy road to 'better and more deliberate' may represent real change in the way ministry is currently structured. If children are never exposed to the 'main' service on Sunday, you might discuss a shift to inclusion through the worship time, or full inclusion on the first or last Sunday of the month.

As you know, change isn't always an easy pill to swallow. Dr. Henry Cloud writes, "We change our behavior when the pain of staying the same becomes greater than the pain of changing. Consequences give us the pain that motivates us to change."[14]

And it's not just a matter of adding one more task and objective. It may mean changing structure for existing events to allow for better access to multiple generations. You might tap the Encore Generation to serve at the children's awards banquet, or have the youth take orders and serve older adults in an after-church lunch.

Once the resolve is in place, you're off to a good start. Continue to cross-pollinate between generational groups, purposefully look for ways to serve one another, and take incremental steps to build relationships. Simply getting older and younger in the same room together may represent progress, but don't rest on your laurels. Find ways to initiate meaningful, helpful dialogue.

I shared locally at Regeneration Church's adult-brunch event. A pair of middle school students hosted the older adults at each round table. In addition to serving beverages and clearing plates, these students came well prepared to guide our table conversations. The students asked open-ended questions about their elders' teenage years, listened intently, and then followed up with further responses and questions that showed they were interested and engaged.

As a visiting guest speaker passionate about uniting generations, I left that day so touched and impressed by the sincere, mature love shown by these middle school hosts and the adults as well.

Vertically Challenged

If you have significant gaps in your vertical relationships, up and down the age scale, perhaps address it first in a diverse-aged leadership team. Then, it could be that your church has no leadership currently focusing on ministry to and through adults in life's second half. Or, maybe your church leadership 'teams' consist of just one individual or couple.

We commonly hear leaders point to a lack of bandwidth when they say 'no' to opportunity. They may not have a team, or their leadership team may not yet be broad or resourceful enough. So, building a strong team and adding to its breadth can better enable you to say 'yes' more often. It's a strategic starting point.

If you attend a large church, it may sometimes feel like a ten-story building, each floor housing a decade. Those on the higher floors always take the elevator, and those on the lower floors generally take the stairs and rarely even see the older folks on the elevator. The lower floors enjoy the exercise, hate elevator music, and confess to feeling a little awkward interacting with those from outside their *lower floor* cultures.

But we don't want to invest our time in building a better elevator when the whole analogy of the church as a ten-story building should fall flat.

Depending on degrees of generational separation with the church, though, let's think of this as a *bridge-building* assignment. And the bridges want to welcome two-way traffic, moving north and south along the age corridor.

Simply put, this is also a *family-building* enterprise. Unless our own family has a high degree of dysfunction, we don't typically refer to different generations within our family as 'our side' and 'their side'.

Vive La Différence

Volumes have captured the subtle and not so elusive nuances of each distinct, US living generation. One such book—a very helpful resource—is *The Intergenerational Church* by Pete Menconi[15], currently serving on the YES! board of directors.

Significant life events have marked each of us at pivotal points in our development; this book helps us recognize and appreciate some of these generational differences.

And Pete highlights the contrast between *multi*-generational churches and those that are very intentionally *inter*generational. '*Multi*' may mean all the generational puzzle pieces are in the box, but '*inter*' means you've begun intentionally connecting those pieces together.

Genetically, our personalities are wired differently. Our birth orders, family dynamics, parenting, grandparenting, church upbringing, peer influence, and other social environs have all left their imprints. We want neither to exaggerate these differences nor ignore them.

Sometimes one church group makes a valiant attempt to close generation gaps. For example, the older adults invite their high school students to a friendly Friday night putt-putt competition followed by complimentary pizza. But if they approached the event without input from the students with whom they're trying to connect, something gets lost in translation.

Most of the students opt to attend their school's basketball game that same evening, and the warm, generation-connecting gesture becomes awkwardly disappointing, with just three home school students participating. The effort, then, is often short-lived, and they soon crawl back into their generational cocoon, convinced other generations just aren't all that interested in making connections.

Think about it. You are on this side of the river and want to build a bridge to the other side. If the other side has no human habitation, collaboration isn't possible.

But here we are talking about **real people** on the river's other side, people with a similar stake in the success of your church. To each other you may be distant, barely visible, somewhat threatening silhouettes.

So, a natural first step in moving toward greater understanding and cross-generational relationships is to **invite other generations to your leadership table**—even if in the beginning, only for "extra" church events.

Making the First Move

People tend to support what they help create. This simple principle is so important and so often overlooked.

The impetus for moving more deliberately toward intergenerational ministry may come from the lead pastor, who hopefully has a heart for the whole body and a birds-eye view of dynamics between generations in the church—be they healthy, silent, quiet, awkward or strained.

The desire for change may come from those overseeing children or youth ministry. Through national training resources, they are likely learning more about how vital it is for their kids/students to interact more with mature adults beyond their peer group. While kids may instinctively turn to Google or their peers for quick answers, these can be shallow conduits for transferring wisdom and discernment.

Openness to change may emerge from those who lead ministry with the Encore Generation. Or, it can easily come from the middle—young married couples realizing they need some older mentors in their lives—or perhaps from Baby Boomers and Generation X, not ready to identify exclusively with adults who are older and who want friendships with those younger as well. While many are thrilled to have parts of child-rearing come to an end, no one wants to feel obsolete.

The desire for more non-peer relationships is likely already simmering, perhaps quietly suppressed or sometimes loudly expressed. Churches need leaders who help carve suitable paths for these relationships. But it takes intentional approaches to get there.

Movie night? A study of how Millennials approach life, complete with their participation in a panel discussion? Prayer partnerships? Women serving as mentor moms in a MOPS [16] (Mothers of Preschoolers) group? Reverse mentoring with the young teaching the older about technology? Visualize what might lead to stronger, healthier relationships between generations.

Eyes on the Prize

No matter who gets the ball rolling, let's reaffirm that we're looking for a **kingdom-minded win for all generations**. It's not all about our own generation's need that initially stirred our heart and brought us to the conversation.

Don't let needs of just one generation dominate the discussion. We all lose when generations drift apart, and we all win when the Body comes together in unity.

When I hear young adults at our church's prayer meetings openly share their personal struggles, I see how astronomically problems can escalate within today's young peer culture. Surrounded by easy access to drugs that I never encountered, some face life-and-death struggles. How I wish another Christian adult or I had intervened earlier to steer them in another direction! But I'm also grateful to pray with them fervently, knowing God heals and transforms.

Ideally, the lead pastor will catch a vision for stronger ministry *between* generations. While he or she may not always be the earliest adopter, the lead pastor is in the best position to bring every generation to the leadership table. Your pastor can facilitate a cohesive, ongoing effort, bolstered by Sunday sermons as well, such as the following:

- A topical series that sheds spiritual light on the four or five generations in your church, focused on a single generation each Sunday. In addition to educating the congregation on that generation's key trademarks, bring into focus an individual or couple from your church representing that specific generation, and draw parallels from Scripture (e.g. correlate the prophet Nehemiah with the Builder generation).
- An exegetical sermon on Titus 2 or Malachi 4:6.
- Teaching about the interdependent nature of the Body of Christ and the Family of God.

And for added reinforcement, consider LIVE short interviews at different times from a generational mix—child, teenager, college student, young parent, mid-age or second-half adult—fresh examples of how they shared their faith, saw prayers answered, went on missions trips, or lived intentionally and reached those outside their peer group. These can often lead to dynamic discussions in the church lobby following a service. More important, healthier, cross-generational relationships may emerge.

Your efforts will rise and fall with leadership. If your lead pastor and church board never become enthusiastic drivers in this initiative, it will not likely get the full traction it deserves. As one respected leader told me, "Departmental fixes won't suffice; you need buy-in from the lead pastor."

The book *Sticky Faith*[17] by Dr. Kara Powell and Dr. Chap Clark from the Fuller Youth Institute points dramatically to the failure of our silo approaches in youth ministry. A more recent release from the Fuller Youth Institute, *Growing Young*[18], further reinforces the importance of intergenerational engagement. Leaders of children or youth who have read these books may already be pumped to help bridge generations more deliberately. More on that in a later chapter.

Snapshots of well-attended youth meetings—gatherings that typically combine fun and craziness with worship and Bible study—can look healthy in the short-term. But without deeper relationship with a broader cross-section of spiritually mature Christians, the spiritual fallout rate as these kids graduate from high school is alarming.

So, many children and youth leaders have a growing understanding of this need from their side of the river, while older adult leaders may see how desperately older adults need an infusion of broader purpose. The food at their seniors-only potluck is growing stale.

Enlisting New Leaders

What's beautiful about moving down this path toward greater collaboration between generations is that **the need is real**, and **the calling is firmly rooted in Scripture**.

We are the **Body** of Christ and the **family** of God. Both metaphors and the Biblical references surrounding them stress the *interdependent* nature of each part of the body or family.

Market segmentation might be a good tactic if we're called to be the *Business of Christ*, but this isn't where Scripture leads us. *Divide and conquer* strategies are designed to weaken and defeat an enemy—not to bring unity within the Church.

Leaving people out of conversations is not the best way to move toward unity. As Peter Drucker once said, "Not to consult is to insult."[19]

If our goal were to move toward a stronger intercultural mix, we'd quickly agree that appointing ten Caucasians to address the issue might not be our wisest move.

So, what do we do if we still have generational gaps at the leadership table?

Getting previously disconnected joints back in their socket can help create movement and interest. For second half adult leadership, **even starting with one individual leader outside your targeted age group** is a healthy step forward. And one often leads to another; the Thirty Something brings along his/her friend, and that friend joins the team. Realize that an incomplete leadership team can leave gaps of perspective, so keep at it over time until each generation is represented, engaging a mix of both staff and laity.

Where do we find people with passion to drive this generation-to-generation emphasis?

Look for leaders who already experience the value or who have perhaps experienced the pain when cross-generational unity is lacking.

Young adults with strong relationships with their grandparents may be good candidates. At a church in Washington, we noticed Jarred, a 19-year-old student deeply engaged in conversation with a man in his seventies. We asked if the gentleman was his grandpa. "Yes, I have several grandpas in this church!" he said, smiling broadly.

Consider including a mature teenager or young adult on your team.

At the other end of the age spectrum, we recommend identifying mid-age and older adults who have stayed engaged with younger generations, perhaps those involved in discipling new believers or those already engaged in teaching, mentoring, coaching, or counseling younger people.

Gauging Girth

Following are tabulation exercises to help you evaluate the generational breadth of your team. It's not an affirmative action initiative, but its blanks can alert us to potential gaps in perspective. For instance, I can check boxes only in half of the categories ahead. To keep it simple, you can include stepchildren and step-grandchildren in your children/ grandchildren tally:

Grandchild with _____ Living Grandparent(s)

Son or Daughter with _____ Living Parent(s)

✓   **Son- or Daughter-in-Law** with __2__ Living Parent(s)-in-Law

Parent with _____ Child(ren) Still Living at Home

✓   **Parent** with __4__ Adult Child(ren) Living Outside the Home

✓   **Parent-in-Law** with __4__ Child(ren)-in-Law

✓   **Grandparent** with __4__ Grandchild(ren)

Great Grandparent with _____ Great-Grandchild(ren)

Besides focusing on current family relationships, your team's depth can be further measured by **loss**. Who on your team has experienced such a loss?

Grandparent — Parent — Child — Spouse — Sibling — Grandchild — Great-Grandchild

On the marriage spectrum, who falls into these categories?

Single   Single Again (thru death/divorce)   **Married   Married Again**

These simple exercises may remind you that all of your current team members are married, and none have a living grandparent. You could downplay your homogeneity by acknowledging you were all previously single, and you still have fond and vivid memories of your grandparents. But a single person with living grandparents might bring a fresh, needed viewpoint. Also bringing valuable perspective are those who have lost loved ones, suffered the pain of divorce, or fought serious illness.

As you form or reshape your team, don't be too quick to jump immediately into solutions and new program ideas. Keep initial conversations at the need level.

How significant is your church's need for better connections between generations? Where is ministry between generations already working well? Where is it not working? What is the net effect of leaving the status quo unchecked?

It is essential to value input from every generation represented at the table. It probably won't take long before someone expresses a thought that builds up his or her own generation, while subtly putting down another.

These are opportune teaching moments that can help highlight the need for greater understanding between generations.

On this journey to better collaboration, encourage your team in their listening skills, especially when you're on completely different pages. *"I completely disagree with you, but I'm listening. Tell me more."*—reflects an honest, non-defensive posture and the kind of attitude you want to encourage.

HALF TWO — DAY FIVE

This Land has some interesting bridges and towers. And we're quickly discovering that some of the most enriching and helpful conversations take place on the bridges, just down the road from the towers.

From Generation to Generation

The New Testament is full of wonderful examples of effective, strategic intergenerational relationships. Spend time looking at the dynamics between Paul/Timothy or Paul/Titus.

Titus 2 is a great example of movement up and down the age ladder. Paul **the older** instructs Titus **the younger** to teach **the older**, so that they in turn will influence **the younger**.

And these relationships are not random anomalies that we conveniently set aside as happenstance or as irrelevant to our culture. About three quarters of Paul's letters begin with intergenerational relationships. And I contend that parts of this intergenerational paradigm, particularly the young teaching the older, were even more radical back in Paul's era and paternalistic culture.

When your team has a growing sense of the value of generation-to-generation ministry, you can then begin charting a more intentional course at your church. Because each church is unique, don't simply download our or someone else's playbook. **Learn from others and prayerfully prepare a game plan that dovetails with the unique mission of your church and the special opportunities present in your community.**

With multiple generations at the table committed to stepping outside their own comfort zones, you'll have a unique opportunity to create programs and events that take multiple perspectives into account. You can quickly rule out lame options that sound good to one generation only.

As your new or generationally enhanced team begins meeting, offer free food and/or meet somewhere neutral, with good eye contact opportunity. Keep looking for common ground that will gain enthusiastic support and traction—from both sides of the river.

To help see others in a different light, you might suggest a combined talent night, with performances alternating between younger and older, then capping off with age-blended performances. If one side of the river thinks this is a really bad idea, paddle together downstream to something better.

On your church calendar, don't simply tack an intergenerational ministry event on top of an already busy schedule. Start with something already on your docket that you can now transform into ministry that intentionally crosses generational lines. Invite teenagers or college students to speak on a panel about 'things they love and things they don't understand about older adults' in your adult class. This exercise will likely be an energetic, eye-opening icebreaker.

And then don't stop with the events themselves. Focus on how each of you can formally or informally become a catalyst for more meaningful interaction beyond your generation. Begin modeling it as leaders. Challenge yourself:

- My career was in _____, so how can I use my expertise to help those younger/older?
- I have always loved music, but I need someone younger to explain the _____?
- I love fishing, but how can I ask a couple of young guys to spend a day fishing with me?

The end target is a thriving church where artificial age boundaries do not limit our expressions of God's love. **We can't settle for generations simply tolerating each other or exchanging occasional pleasantries.** Yearn for them to develop a deep love for those outside their peer group, cheering them on. We have so much to learn from each other.

From the lips of Jesus in John 13:35 (NLT), *Your love for one another will prove to the world that you are my disciples.* Without this kind of intentional love and collaboration, we sadly see multi-generational churches with *Tolerate & Mediate* environments or shrinking age demographics because of *Grumble & Go* generational migration.

As we conclude this chapter, I recommend that churches tag a specific leader to help their churches stay on course regarding intergenerational ministry.

It's quite a responsibility. Perhaps you are that visionary person. While ministry between generations should ideally be part of everyone's ministry emphasis, someone needs to champion the cause continually, making sure it stays in clear focus.

Consider how your church's mission gets accomplished, not just separately through each age group, but together through intentional, cross-generational relationships.

If we let American culture (even American *church* culture) prevail, with our proclivity to generational segregation, intentional ministry *between* generations can easily slide to the back burner—or off the stove and out of the kitchen completely.

For years churches have invested heavily in separating generations. Some of this makes sense in moderation, addressing specialized needs in each life stage. But we've gone overboard and have set some strong Biblical models aside, settling too often for peer-only ghettos.

We all share a common need for meaningful connections both inside *and outside* our peer groups, and our faith is to be transmitted from *generation to generation*. **'Generation to generation' is not simply a way to mark the passing of time; it's a context and strategy for passing our faith.**

Lord, help us lead effectively as we invest some of our best energies to bring generations together for your glory.

✓ Beyond simply tabulating your church's generational demographics, do you have a core of people who see the need for stronger relationships *between* generations?

✓ Do you see the importance of this in God's economy, or is it simply an optional approach among many approaches? Is there enough will and determination— with God's help—to drive the change?

✓ When did you first realize you could influence those older, not just peers and younger?

✓ Can you think of one young leader right now who might join you in serving, inspiring, and mobilizing the Encore Generation? You don't need half a dozen to get started —you need only one. Consider taking that person out for coffee or a milkshake to explore ministry possibilities. This could influence that young person significantly and revolutionize your second half adult group.

Day 6. EXCHANGE RATE

Moving Beyond Half-Hearted Investment

Teach the older men to exercise self-control,
to be worthy of respect, and to live wisely.
They must have sound faith and be filled with love and patience.
Titus 2:2 (NLT)

JUST WEEKS INTO LAUNCHING YES, we sought counsel from a respected leader in second half adult ministry.

One of his first golden nuggets was, ***"Don't quit your day job."*** He further explained that pastors and church leaders will graciously affirm how important older adults are in their churches, but in reality, they are usually four or five down in the generational pecking order, and church budgets barely reach that far.

Some may want to dabble in this ministry, but it often sees less than optimal results.

However, Judy and I were already in; we had both left our day jobs and were pursuing this new ministry adventure full-time. While confident that God had called both of us, we also know to seek wisdom through an abundance of counselors. We acknowledged this leader's truth, giving us clear and fair warning. But the half-hearted investment he referenced was part of what tugged at our hearts and drew us in.

Out on a Limb

We already faced a financial dilemma in pursuing God's call. To make matters more challenging, we stepped out by faith in 2008, one of the more financially dismal years for our nation.

Our ministry friend added, "As you know, churches more commonly set their hearts on reaching young families. Older adults and the broader scope of families (beyond parent-child) more often land outside the church leaders' radar. Leaders figure these adults have walked with the Lord for decades and are okay on autopilot, equipped to fend for themselves until they become frail. These churches may set aside funds for a part-time care pastor assigned to visit shut-ins, oversee hospital visitations, and conduct memorial services."

Admittedly, we're a bit stubborn in our faith. Ten years earlier we had moved our family of six to California's central coast, responding similarly to God's call while encountering parallel words of caution. Some rightfully questioned our sanity when I accepted a cut in salary to leave secular employment and work at Bethany College, an institution with a long, colorful history of outstanding educational/ministry preparation—but also of financial instability.

Bethany, just minutes away from the Silicon Valley, was in a community where real estate prices far outpaced those of the Southern California city we were leaving. One of Judy's brothers wondered aloud if we were putting our four kids on the Titanic.

Now here we were ten years later, both of us again committing to serve in an arena full of exciting potential but also fraught with external doubt-and-insecurity perceptions—and half-hearted investment.

We both had chosen to serve full-time but to share a single, non-guaranteed salary, at far less than I had been making at the fledgling college. And, although our new board had set our modest salary, it existed only on paper as part of the minutes of our first meeting. We would still have to raise our own support.

As mentioned earlier, our home church was extremely gracious and generous in helping us launch *YES! Young Enough to Serve*—for the first six months. Honestly, going forward after that was a monumental struggle. We faced mounting debt as support trickled in. We plodded on with firm resolve and confidence—most days. On days when my faith wavered, Judy stood strong. And when she wondered if we were going to make it, I encouraged her.

When we heard older adults complaining about their fixed incomes, we were slightly jealous. Our remuneration was sporadic; it needed to be fixed, in more ways than one.

Deep and Wide

We were committed then (and still are) to keeping *YES! Young Enough to Serve* interdenominational. The needs and patterns we observe are not tied to doctrinal nuances and exist in a wide array of denominational and non-denominational churches. Still, Judy and I have strong ties with the Assemblies of God, and several friends recommended that we pursue United States missionary status with the AG.

We proposed the idea to our interdenominational YES! board of directors. A board member who attends a thriving Baptist church was completely supportive, offering this wise counsel to the full board: "Let's go as deep as we can with the Assemblies of God and as broad as we can with other churches."

So, with our board's support, we cast out the net to the AG missionary administrative leaders. We weren't quite sure how they would respond to our interdenominational commitment. Their kingdom-minded response, however, was refreshing. "As long as you don't exclude the Assemblies of God churches in the mix, we are completely supportive."

We then went through a rigorous process to qualify as US missionary candidates. During our missionary training, we learned that one of the biggest temptations we would face as we raised support was part-time employment. "Other employment will divide your interest, tether you geographically, and could permanently keep you from addressing your broader and deeper ministry goals." Within a month after hearing this warning, I had five tempting part-time job offers, which I respectfully, and somewhat painfully, declined.

Later, as financial support reached a minimum threshold, we became our denomination's second appointed US missionary couple [20] to focus on adults over fifty, commissioned to help churches better steward their serving and disciple-making potential. Surprising to some but consistent with our mission, significant support came from outside the US, outside our denomination, and outside the 50+ age demographic we target.

After our appointment as missionaries, we shared with the seniors group at my home church, Life Center, in Tacoma, Washington, where I grew up. Flooded with emotion, I reflected on the many adults in that church who had nurtured my faith when I was younger.

As a child, I had memorized the names of all the missionaries our church supported and prayed for each of them by name every night. And now, Judy and I were among the missionaries for whom others were praying.

My heart for missions, the broader family of God, and older adults had been strongly nurtured there in Tacoma, even going back to my elementary school years. A dear Presbyterian widow, Mrs. Fredericks, led an after-school Bible club and frequently shared prayer requests from missionaries. One such request from Asia somehow lodged in my heart, and for years I would end my childhood prayers with, *"And help Sung-Hae-Song to know you."* I expect to meet him someday in heaven.

It was after one of these Bible club meetings that I committed my life to Christ at the age of seven, led by another passionate Presbyterian woman, our neighbor Hazel Askren, who recently passed away at the age of 95.

My pastor's brother, Mark Buntain, was an incredibly anointed missionary serving in Calcutta, India. He and other missionaries preached often at our church and stirred our hearts toward missions.

As a teenager, I remember kneeling beside my bed, sensing that God was calling me to be a missionary, specifically to help build churches. My dad was a building contractor, and at that time, I thought God might be calling me to build physical church structures in other countries. Yet construction and I didn't mesh particularly well, and I could later see that God was preparing me over the next four decades to help build churches—in a different way, apart from brick and mortar, and right here in the United States.

Judy and I now serve as US missionaries under the umbrella of Church Development, helping to revitalize American churches. In my mid-fifties, I had finally stepped into this special missionary calling God had placed on my heart as a teen.

The idea that the US needs missionaries is foreign to some. *Real* missionaries invest their lives in *other* nations. Thankfully, other countries are also burdened for the United States and are sending missionaries here.

When I asked an adult class whether the US needed missionaries, one adult answered in the affirmative, but added, "Because so many foreigners are moving here."

In response I asked, "Is that why America sends missionaries around the world? Are we chasing down relocated Americans?" No!

The US has incredible Christian roots. It is and has always been a tremendous missionary-sending nation; however, that's not to say we are spiritually healthy and need only target the huddled masses arriving on our shores.

We live today in a post-Christian culture in need of missionaries, evangelists, and other prophetic voices to help spiritually reawaken our country. Our nation's significant role in global missions will diminish if we ignore the home front.

Perhaps you too experienced a special call from God much earlier in life, one that has percolated for decades. Spend time praying about that. It may be shaped differently from your initial plan, but it could still be part of His plan for you. You are still *young enough to serve*.

I share this bit of personal history also as a backdrop for what we've observed with church leaders across the nation. Despite a burgeoning older adult population, most churches and denominations still approach this amazing untapped Half Two potential with half-hearted investment:

- Little or no allocated budget.
- Benign programs that seem to pacify rather than mobilize and equip.
- Part-time leadership at every level (church, district,

nationally) — often serving without compensation.

But, in the midst of this haze, God gave us signs that we were on a good path, and He spoke similarly to others in this crusade for change.

In the final analysis, we can't spend the **second** or **last** half of life complaining about being **second** or **last** — or settling for **half**-heartedness. None of us wants to reach our last days and have it said about us that he/she *did what was right in the eyes of the LORD, but not wholeheartedly.* 2 Chronicles 25:2 (NIV)

Halving the Heart

On the revenue side, we've seen way too many churches sign their death warrant by fostering environments increasingly hostile to older adults. These seasoned saints are often the church's financial backbones, and body pain multiplies when discs degenerate, slip, bulge, or herniate. An older adult mass exodus may bring short-term emotional relief to a young pastor in skinny jeans, but economic upheaval and insolvency could be around the corner.

How sad, though, if we pass out earplugs and sympathetically prop older adults up *only* so the lights can stay on. As our *not-so-subtle* friend Chuck Stecker[21] puts it, "We treat older adults as though they are culturally irrelevant — except for their ability to spell the word *tithe.*"

On the other side of the coin, adults who threaten to take their toys and go home if they don't get their own way can create other untenable situations.

So how do we break through these half-hearted investment realities without a lot of moaning, complaining, and conniving?

If Half Two ministry is simply about older Christians gathering together to support one another, we unintentionally paint ourselves into a corner. Outsiders are inclined to see limited, internalized, and fading potential—ending with death.

In America, faced with the choice of either supporting young people or supporting older adults, we almost always deem the younger generations worthier for long-term investment. If we who are older settle too deeply and exclusively into second half circles, we're likely to perpetuate half-hearted investment.

Churches that over-emphasize adult leisure activities can also unwittingly reinforce stereotypes of ministry-neutral, self-sufficient retirees led out to pasture, blissfully enjoying their sunset years. We know some good ministry still happens in that context, but it's not something most churches feel justified in lavishly supporting. Church boards tend to say, "Let them pay their own way for fun, food, fellowship, and field trips."

Sometimes we give mixed signals. Which is it? Do we want our church to expect more or less of us? Many seasoned adults think they're in the off-season and self-sufficient. Some church finance committees are happy to go along with this assumption and give 50+ ministries unseasonably low budgets.

Outside businesses may step into this financial vacuum and reinforce the leisurely path. Travel agents tempt cash-strapped, second-half adult leaders, "If you can get twenty adults to join you, we'll cover the cost of a Caribbean cruise for you and your spouse—and we'll throw in a side trip to Disney World, too."

And overworked and underpaid Half Two leaders feel like they've won the lottery—without even buying a ticket.

Third world problems and unreached people groups, too, will certainly be more compelling than older American adults already reached with the gospel—especially when we fail to see any connection between the two. But if the definition of Americans *finishing well* gets tied to *finishing wells* in Africa, people are more apt to value both.

Many reliable studies show that spiritual conversions become rarer as people grow older. For surveyed members of the National Association of Evangelicals[22], respondents became Christians at the average age of 13. In this survey, only two percent reported conversions after age 30.[23]

Other studies yield different but roughly similar results. Christians may interpret their salvation points differently, depending on their theological understandings. Some adults with a reawakened faith well after thirty may still point to their infant baptism as synonymous with their initial commitment to Christ, skewing age statistics downward.

Rather than marshaling greater resources for the stiffer challenge, these statistics can also lead to scarcer investment in Half Two ministry. True, it is more difficult to touch people with the Good News when they have been set in their ways for so many years. But we've also seen explosive power coming from people who commit their lives to Christ beyond the age of fifty. They are eager to make up for lost time and turn their world right side up.

The *Not Too Late* Years

At 58, Patricia Keough from Sparks, Nevada committed her life to Jesus. Her stepson led her into a relationship with Christ shortly after her husband passed away. Since then, nearly her whole family has come to Christ. Pat continues to grow more confident in sharing her faith, recently experiencing the first-time joy of leading someone from outside her family to Christ.

For over two decades, Pat has been significantly engaged in her home church, Crosswinds, starting with a *New Beginnings* class at the age of sixty. She now hosts a small group, helps with *Awana* [24] (children's ministries) on Wednesday nights, feeds women at the local mission, visits a couple nursing homes monthly, and attends *Vintage Life* social events, women's conferences and other Bible studies.

Pat sums it up by saying, "In Christ and through my church, I've experienced a whole new life. I'm so much more alive and have something to look forward to *almost* every day!"

We first met Pat in 2016 when she joined us at *Gleanings for the Hungry* [25], boldly embarking on her first missions trip at the age of eighty and returning again a year later.

Like many beyond-fifty converts, Pat shows no signs of complacency, drudgery, or "paid my dues, served my time" in her Christian walk. She personifies the new-creation-in-Christ excitement found in 2 Corinthians 5:17 (NIV), ... *The old has gone, the new is here!*

As we compare statistics and budgets, it's a huge mistake if we perceive ourselves to compete with younger generations. It can't be an either/or proposition. We even have to guard against competition and envy between 50+ generations: currently Generation X, Boomers, and Builders.

As Boomers, we like to see ourselves as world-changers, and we may be too quick to dismiss ministry contributions of generations ahead of us. Builders know they sacrificed to buy the land and build the buildings our churches utilize today and may struggle at times with personal ownership, as framed in Gordon MacDonald's book, *Who Stole My Church?*[26]

God loves every generation, and He wants us to thrive, ourselves, but also love and encourage all generations, not simply our own. And we must become adept in passing batons with finesse to younger generations.

As we've already discussed, generations are not meant to live in isolation. Healthy families enjoy vital relationships that intentionally cross generational lines. Our bodies have highly interdependent parts. The Church, as we know, is both a family and the Body of Christ.

The more we can embrace the role of seasoned adults as **integral to the whole body** and **ambassadors effective in**

reaching those outside the Church, the more churches will invest in Half Two ministries. If we remain half-focused and self-contained, how can we hope for more than partial investment?

HALF TWO — DAY SIX

We're only six days into this trip, and our tour guide's voice is growing hoarse. Time to look for some young, energetic voices to help lead this journey!

On the surface, it's sometimes difficult to see how something positive like self-sufficiency can lead to isolation. This Encore Generation sometimes projects confidence to the point we simply let them be. But, that attitude of self-reliance has unintended consequences.

We all need each other. Each generation needs the attention and investment of the broader body of Christ.

Too Old to Fly Solo

We have also set the stage for shallow investment by almost exclusively seeking older "retired" leaders to lead second half adult ministry. It may seem financially prudent to hire a spiritually mature, part-time leader who qualifies for Social Security/Medicare and who may also be drawing a pension. We can get more bang for our buck, right?

We can't keep doing this alone. If we don't allow the next generations into the cockpit, who will fly the plane when we're incapacitated or gone? We need the gift of fresh eyes.

What about hiring **a younger Titus, Timothy, or Tabitha for Half Two leadership**? We might happily have to consider a full-time hire with medical benefits and a salary commensurate with children and youth ministry leaders. Too often, we've set the expectation bar and budget too low.

However, churches might see strategic value in moving beyond the tiny sliver they've been allocating for this area of ministry, especially when they see the potential fruit of their efforts:

- Stronger intergenerational engagement,
- Vital inclusion of Generation X and Boomers,
- More energy and creativity,
- More outreach and intentional disciple-making,
- Revitalized prayer emphasis engaging all generations,
- Spiritually dynamic grandparenting,
- Proactive protection from scams and other forms of elder abuse,
- Numeric growth,
- Increased support for caregivers,
- Improved use of discretionary time,
- Igniting of life-redeeming encore careers,
- Strengthened partnership with missionaries,
- Better stewardship of accumulated resources,
- Stronger giving.

It's exciting to reflect on Paul's wisdom in assigning younger leaders such as Titus and Timothy to teach older men and women. It wasn't a fluke. There was and is a ton of godly wisdom behind this counter-intuitive, interdependent strategy.

Some people talk passionately about the Titus 2 model but highlight only Part B, teaching older men and women to live lives that positively impact younger generations. They sometimes forget Part A, where it's Paul the Elder asking Titus the Younger to do this teaching.

Is it a mistake to hire Half Two leaders in their seventies or eighties? We know many wonderfully competent, energetic and collaborative leaders over seventy who fulfill this role beautifully. It has also become a familiar landing spot for former lead pastors with a passion to continue leading. It would, of course, be disingenuous for *YES! Young Enough to Serve* to argue against the viability of older leaders in key leadership roles.

On the upside, having a respected older leader on the church staff can be an invaluable source of wisdom and perspective, especially if the rest of the pastoral team is much younger. This works particularly well when the older leaders take an active role in regular ministry staff meetings, and do not allow their part-time status to preempt them from such meetings.

We have concerns, however, when this limited, older age range becomes our singular, automatic *go-to* pool for Half Two ministry leaders. We already must jump some high hurdles to engage adults in their fifties and sixties in '50+ ministry'. For many reasons, the *Young Old* resist digging their cleats into this track, and *50+ ministries* can easily become just the *70+* leg of the race. To be fair, this can happen with younger leaders at the helm, but it's even more common with older leaders.

Sadly, **intergenerational connections haven't been happening often and deeply enough in this older-to-older paradigm.** The adults sing *Great is Thy Faithfulness*[27] with their peer group, take field trips to car museums, enjoy outdoor potlucks, and imagine the future awaiting them in heaven. Programs can get caught in time warps, adding to external perceptions of personal obsolescence. Meanwhile, deliberate opportunities to connect with younger generations and make disciples may be slipping away.

One passionate mother in a Pacific Northwest church underscored the need to move quickly in the intergenerational relationship arena. "Some of our seasoned heroes are about to die, and my kids haven't yet heard their stories. We can't spend months and years just talking about this. We need those conversations and friendships now."

Same Old Same Old

Finally, this older leadership paradigm has become way too predictable a fixture in American church culture. Yes, older adults may sometimes resist being led by someone much younger, and perhaps this biblical idea hasn't yet crossed their minds.

Also, young ministers can fail to consider the refreshing

impact they might have with adults in Half Two. Too often older adults instead become obstacles these younger ministers try to work around—as they attempt to bring the church into the twenty-first century, sometimes thoughtfully and sometimes with little diplomacy.

By contrast, Paul told Titus **first** to teach the older men and women as **a primary approach** to influence younger generations. Are we editing Scripture or allowing Scripture to edit us?

Our Christian colleges and seminaries rarely prepare students for Half Two ministry because the opportunity is so obscure and distant for younger adults. They may get limited exposure to elderly visitation, pastoral care, funeral etiquette, or a course in Adulthood and Aging. But rarely do they get a vision of the dynamic impact **they** might **now** have in the lives of empty nesters, retirees, grandparents, and the broader spectrum of adults over fifty.

Younger adults are beautifully positioned to help bridge the generational divide. They can coach those older in ways to better connect with those younger. They can also more easily rally young people around older adults by modeling younger-to-older ministry themselves.

I've enjoyed ongoing conversations with a handful of Encore Generation leaders currently in their forties, the rare exceptions. They wrestle with similar issues—ageism, music, tight budgets, passivity, entitlement—and they, too, are eager to change this age group's ministry paradigms.

Dan and Shani Parotti from Cedar Valley Church in

Bloomington, Minnesota[28], are one such couple, both in their forties. Not yet in the 50+ age demographic they are serving, they show heartfelt love for their adults. More, they deeply desire to encourage and nourish their serving and disciple-making potential.

As the youngest leader working with second half adults in his denomination's district, Dan considers it helpful to be *"old enough* to understand them, *strong enough* to handle them, *young enough* to inspire younger pastors to see their value, and *inspirational enough* to engage them in church ministry opportunities"—which are often led by younger pastors and lay leaders.

The Parottis and other leaders not yet at the *Highway 50+* onramp have palpable energy and passion. I'm excited about their church's potential to experience greater leadership longevity.

Full Circle

Young leaders often have a strong passion for neglected people groups and are motivated to correct injustices. They know in principle how wrong it is to neglect and devalue any class of people, including older adults.

If youth leaders are quick to ask the Encore Generation to help fund their initiatives and outreaches, make sure their ministry team members later return with stories.

One student shared, "On our Uganda trip, we stopped daily to thank God for those of you back home uplifting us with your prayers and financial support. We did not go there alone. You were there with us as we baptized six new believers on the last night of our trip. Thanks again for the eternal impact you made in my life and the lives of those we served."

The adult leader responded, "Earlier, we appreciated your prompt, handwritten thank you notes for our financial gifts, but it's these firsthand reports of our return on investment that help us see your sincerity even more. You didn't just take the money and run. It's a joy and honor to partner with you financially."

Moving beyond just financial investment, let's help open eyes to the time, skills, wisdom and fervent prayer these Half Two adults can also bring to the table—as co-laborers in Christ. Invite some of these adults to join the youth on the next missions trip.

No matter what their age, Half Two leaders who can assemble a strong age-diverse team to model generational bridge-building can help your church move closer to more generous, whole-hearted investment. A win-win for the kingdom.

An Old Book Full of New Ideas

If we didn't have a significant problem with generational gaps in our culture and churches, and if we didn't have strong New Testament precedents for younger leaders encouraging and challenging older men and women, we might be drawn to other solutions.

Yes, the sick can minister to the sick. Prisoners can encourage each other in their faith. Orphans can minister to orphans. Widows can touch the lives of other widows. Generations can find solace in their peer groups.

But how great when the healthy and free willingly visit the sick and imprisoned. Strong families adopt orphans. Married couples befriend widows. The rich bless the poor. Ethnic majorities give honor to ethnic minorities, and vice versa. Those with courage to step outside their box repeatedly discover that blessings flow in both directions.

Several years ago, a twenty-something female in our church realized that a vibrant church matriarch had never experienced a shower given in her honor. This elder, single saint had hosted numerous showers for other women over the years, but she personally never had a ring or new child to celebrate. With others eager to help, the young lady threw a festive surprise shower one Sunday after church, an afternoon garden party cherished by everyone who attended—and especially by our honored friend.

Too often we deprive ourselves of the rich contrast God intends for us to experience. Like the rich young ruler who sadly walked away from Jesus' admonition to give all he had to the poor, our personal salvation, too, often sits at the opposite end of the color wheel.

We can discover our real need, calling, and deepest satisfaction as we go into messy, uncomfortable, insecure, unhealthy, poor, unjust, and ugly situations. Jesus walked those roads for us. As we focus on Christ's rescue and redemption of others, His redemption comes to us as well.

What a blessing when the young demonstrate genuine concern for those older, and when those older show similar concern for those younger. Now these are ministry paradigms and relationships we can all invest in. **Wholeheartedly.**

- ✓ Do you have influence in your church? Can you raise important questions when you see programs and patterns that seem out of synch with Scripture? If something needs to change, what initial steps can you take to model the change for others?

- ✓ If our own families modeled the cross-generational warmth of our church, would relationships become better or more distant?

- ✓ If you are a leader entrusted with ministry to and through adults in life's second half, can you enlist help from a broader age swath to help you both encourage and challenge your adults? How can you accomplish it?

DESTINATION II.

Half Two—
Make It HIS!

Onward,
FOREWORD to Destination II

Half Two —*Make It HIS!*

Dick and Ruth Foth

WE LOVE THE FACT that this book, *Half Two*, is dedicated to Wes' father-in-law, Don Popineau. Or, as Wes calls him, Papa Don. The section you are about to read, *Make It His*, is easily a biographical snapshot of that wonderful man.

We met Don in April of 1978, when Dick became President of Bethany College in Scotts Valley, California, the alma mater of all five of Don and Peggy's children. The school was vital, but small by college standards. Providing a fine education, but always strapped for monies, it was in a precarious position. Don was an enthusiastic encourager. And, before the next decade was out, Don and Peggy had played a huge role in the life of that college because they believed in making their lives His!

When they found themselves in a place of economic flexibility, they came to live near the campus as volunteers on "their own dime." They didn't come for a week or a month or even—could you believe it—for a year. No. They paid their own ticket to come and do whatever was needed on Bethany's campus for THREE YEARS!

Who does that? People who understand that they play for an Audience of One. They threw themselves into the battle for minds and the shaping of young lives. They joined hands with those of us who felt that calling but also got paid for it. They showed us how to live full-out, every day, with purpose and joy.

This section, *Make It His*, throws down the gauntlet to the reader, not to forget Whose we are. Not to stop living early. Never to stop seeing their lives through the lens of the Kingdom! It suggests a kind of generous purpose that sounds like John Bunyan of Pilgrim's Progress fame: "There was a man and they called him mad; the more he gave, the more he had!"

Wes challenges us always to be players (in the game) and pray-ers (in the biggest arena). These next chapters will be "in your face" in the best possible way.

We really like the chapter on prayer. In a frightening 2013 episode, when Ruth's life hung by a thread, she knew beyond doubt that pray-ers were/are, in fact, First Responders. Wes and Judy's thoughts affirm that truth big-time.

What you are about to read will touch your heart and stretch your mind. Watch out!

Dick and Ruth Foth

Co-Authors, *Known: Finding Deep Friendships in a Shallow World*

DESTINATION II. OVERVIEW

Half Two—*Make It HIS!*

"People who make a difference in the world
are not people who have mastered a lot of things.
They are people who have been mastered
by a very few things that are very, very great."
John Piper[29]

WHILE IT'S COMMON FOR OLDER ADULTS to sometimes feel unwanted and unneeded, the truth is that many people, groups, causes, businesses, and other organizations actively compete for their time and attention.

If you're tech savvy, Facebook and social media want a good chunk of your time on their turf. Google wants you to invest time using their search engines and Gmail. Microsoft and thousands of creative engineers want you to use their software or apps. Amazon wants your Prime attention.

Major networks and cable TV all want to pull you into the latest Breaking News story or to entice you to adopt one or more of their shows as must-see favorites. The question of *"Should I watch TV tonight?"* morphs into *"What do you want to watch tonight?"* And much of daytime television also targets retirees.

Advertisers vie for your attention through a wide variety of channels. We are often unaware of how many times a day we get bombarded. And marketers know repetition is often key to infiltrating our world.

Video games and other games entice us to spend hours trying to defeat a known or invisible opponent. We may compete only with ourselves, or bots, in "harmless" but time-consuming word, card, or number games. Video game addiction can easily touch us all, not simply children and adolescents.

Movie producers tease you to boost their box office ratings. Booksellers want you to buy and read their books. They want talk shows and you to discuss and advertise them.

Some of our distractions still come to us in old-fashioned ways, through radio, our mailboxes, and annoying phone solicitations.

Ministries are not exempt from wanting your time and attention. Churches want you to engage in their community. Parachurch organizations and other nonprofits need your volunteer time for their causes. And I'm aware that reading this book takes time. Thank you.

Sometimes we benefit from needed stimulation, but all too often, subtle manipulation happens. We may also feed a growing assumption that we are entitled to multiple leisure hours in front of a television, movie screen, computer, iPad, or smart phone—or somewhere else less technologically tethered.

Should we simply close the door to these multiple platforms vying for our lives? Or do we prayerfully consider how God wants us to steward our time and resources? Do we realize that even when no money exchanges hands and we're fast-forwarding through commercials, we still give up the precious commodity of time that will never come our way again?

Believe me, I am preaching to myself right now as well as to you.

Do we need time away from the cares of this world to recharge our batteries? Absolutely! Let's just make sure we charge our batteries and avoid inadvertently draining ourselves—so that we have energy for what's important.

Let's make sure we surrender even our leisure to God. He deserves to be Lord of both the ebb and flow of our lives. Surrendering both to Him can add incredible joy and purpose to our lives. He is the Restorer of our souls.

While countless entities here on Planet Earth vie for our attention and time, we have an Audience of One who matters more than all the rest put together. We lose big time if we give Him the cold shoulder, or if we live our final decades like we're off the clock and free of accountability. These moments and years matter to Him, to us, to our peers, and to those younger who need fresh examples of what finishing well looks like.

Most of you will agree with the last paragraph, but we often fail to take the next step—to barter wasted hours for fruitful ones.

Sometimes we're wrestling with fatigue, and we have choices when this happens. Take a nap, grab a second cup of coffee, exercise, or vegetate in front of the TV. If we're short on sleep, a power nap might do us good. Otherwise, we might want to get our blood pumping a bit faster with a brisk walk.

America in Idle

But too often, we might find ourselves choosing cruise control, watching hours of television that neither rejuvenates nor gives rest. Even good television content may be quickly forgotten when we're in that tired state.

Let's talk about that wide-screen elephant in the room. *"Television is the menace that everyone loves to hate but can't seem to live without."* —Paddy Chayevsky[30].

Some of you have your TV-watching completely under control and may not even own a television. But, over the years screens have become larger, resolution sharper, colors more vivid, and program choices and recording options limitless—enticing many of us, young and old, to watch more TV than we should.

Even the costs of cable or satellite TV have swelled, making some of us oddly feel we'd be poor stewards not to watch more. The cost per hour goes down the more we watch.

Move through your recording list to your fourth favorite show, if you have one. Would it rock your world to delete it from your record menu and give it up?

Parents give their children a specific amount of "screen

time." Adults can do the same for themselves. Could you restrict yourself to a two-hour viewing max per day?

Consider reducing the number of TVs at your residence. You may want to remove them from bedrooms, or move them from a living room to a den. Television has also migrated to our computers, tablets, and smart phones, but you can choose not to import these TV app portals—or delete them if already there.

You may want to multi-task while watching a favorite TV program, by walking on a treadmill or jogging in place. Get your Fitbit up to those ten thousand daily steps—a much healthier way to watch television.

A couple of times our family completely gave up TV-watching for a month, once with four kids in the home and again later as empty nesters. We quickly discovered many more hours in our days. And, I confess, only two months of TV detox in the last quarter century is probably not enough.

You may want to consider a TV blackout during certain hours of the evening when you could be more productive, like 6 to 8 pm. And when welcomed visitors enter your home for friendship and conversation, don't just mute the TV; shut it off. As with other technologies, our devices—not people—keep us from being fully present in the moment.

As God directs, you may even decide to cut your cable and remove your television completely. But then you'll have another decision—what to do with all the money you save. The Joshua Becker[31] family did it, and he lived to tell, "It will change your family's life forever overnight. It changed ours."

Some of us feel we'd miss out on too much, that we might become clueless in certain conversations, less socially aware. My wife Judy didn't have a TV in their home until she reached high school. She and her four brothers are some of the most sociable and engaging people I know.

Slaying Tougher Dragons

Your life-consuming villains and potential addictions may be something completely different, possibly more destructive and disruptive, like alcohol, online gaming, drugs, or pornography. Earlier euphoric missteps toward freedom counterfeits have saddled you with heavy weights and bondage. Jesus wants to liberate you from sin's grip, and you will need His supernatural help to break free.

It's not too late to raise your hand for help. Your family and this world need you. Consider counseling, a twelve-step program, *Celebrate Recovery*[52], or a residential program like *Teen Challenge*[53].

Even if you have tried unsuccessfully in the past to overcome serious addiction, God wants to help you slay these dragons. Get the help you need. You know a Band-Aid will not suffice; you need deep repentance. Other advice in this book and elsewhere will seem shallow if you don't first deal with these significant core issues.

Substitute Teaching

Moving on from our time-robbing hindrances, let's now

consider how we might find better substitutes for those "free" hours—ways to show God's love more deliberately. Pray about what you might do with that extra hour or two each day:

- Volunteer at a homeless shelter or a crisis pregnancy center.
- Offer to babysit.
- Visit housebound adults.
- Bake cookies for the youth group.
- Serve veterans at your local veteran's hall.
- Coach softball.
- Help teenagers learn to sew, and make dresses for *Dress a Girl Around the World*[34].
- Distribute Bibles with *Gideons International*[35].
- Run for public office.
- Memorize Scripture, take piano lessons, or learn a new language.
- Volunteer with *Prison Fellowship*[36].
- Lead or host a small group.
- Reach out and help a caregiver.
- Become a *Big Brother or Big Sister*[37].
- Serve on the board of PTA or your neighborhood association.
- Play your guitar at a nearby rest home.[38]
- Serve with *Meals on Wheels*[39].
- Engage in *Stephen Ministry*[40] through your church.
- Take a grandchild to the beach.

- Invite your neighbors over for a meal.
- Provide pet care for a friend going on a missions trip.
- Wash your wife's car—oh no, mine will read this!

You may already be an incredible steward of time and can teach the rest of us. We all get 24 hours each day, but some of us have fewer days left. Let's make the most of them.

In my early Azusa Pacific graduate school days, I hitchhiked from California to Washington. To get from Northern California to Oregon, I hopped a freight train and was quickly joined by five bedraggled men, with considerable train-hopping pedigree. This was in the dark ages before smart phones. One man proudly told me he didn't carry a map or wear a watch. "I don't care where I'm going or when I get there," he added.

As Albert Einstein advised, "Make things as simple as possible, but not simpler." When or if I retire, I still want to care about where I'm going, when I get there—and for Whom I am living.

Day 7. ROYAL TREATMENT

Thy KiNGDOM Come

"I know the plans I have for me,"
says the empty nester and retiree.

AS COMMITTED CHRISTIANS, most of us readily affirm God's authority over our lives, both in the present and in the life to come. We have surrendered ourselves to Christ and want Him to rule and reign. Of course, there is a lot of push and pull between our will and God's will, and our sinful nature rears its ugly head more often than we like to admit. We know we need to daily pick up our cross to follow Him.

KiNGDOM vs. kIngdom

English is the only language that capitalizes the personal pronoun in its singular form. "I" wasn't always so tall until someone many centuries ago decided the lowercase "i" looked too puny and inconsequential by itself. The small letter "a" had more bulk and was allowed to stay in its short and pudgy form as a single-letter standalone.

121

I never forget to capitalize "I", but I honestly don't know whether God's "kingdom" is supposed to be capitalized. Some say it should be as a proper noun, but most Bible translations leave it in lowercase.

Ironically, in our practical lives, God's kingdom often gets spelled with a lowercase "k" and is then followed by an uppercase "I." This upper and lowercase tension surfaces often as Christians get close to or enter the empty nest and retirement.

We believe in God's kingdom, but we finally reach a stage when we can define life on our own terms. No earthly boss directing our daytime hours, no kids needing a ride to soccer practice, and no mortgage lender breathing down our necks. We have become our own bosses—kings and queens of our domain.

Sure, we know Who really is boss, and we'll genuinely give Him honor as King. We may pray before meals and at bedtime, read the Word faithfully, tithe regularly, and do our best to stay away from sinful behavior. But in between these margins, there is a good chance our culture's views on retirement and later life are subtly and significantly influencing us—both before and after we reach these life stages.

What primary entitlement signals does our American culture regularly beam to empty nesters and retirees?

- This is the 'self-accountability' zone. This is your time. You're off the clock. You are in control. Say "yes" only when you want to. You are now accountable only to you.

- This is the 'no judgment' zone. *Want to serve others?* Great! *Want to live for yourself?* Great. Whatever floats your boat.
- This is the 'no pressure' zone. You are officially authorized to stay away from anything potentially stressful.
- This is the 'no commitment' zone. You want to be free to roam, so avoid committing to anything that might tie you down.
- This is the 'leisure and entertainment' zone, a season to enjoy the fruit of your labor. So stop, kick back and enjoy. You deserve it.
- This is the 'no rebuke' zone. Save correction for disobedient children, wayward teens, or unfaithful young married couples. *'Respect your elders'* means we should bite our tongue and overlook your faults.
- This is the 'post-development' zone. Your personal growth season is far behind you. You're in the over-the-hill life stage. You can't teach old dogs new tricks. You'll do well to slow your decline.

Zip-a-Dee-Doo-Dah

While we might reject a few of the above messages, chances are good that some of these familiar tunes play quietly in the back of our minds.

Although the volume of discretionary time in retirement doesn't usually measure up to pre-retirement expectations, retirees on average have about three times the discretionary hours as someone employed full-time. And *discretionary* can often get interpreted as, "It's my time, and I'll spend it any way I please."

As Christians, we're a little more tactful and don't necessarily speak "hedon-ese." But we have a fluent understanding of hedonism, allowing some of it to attach to the neurons in our brain. We may even subconsciously use it as a litmus test in our decision-making. We'll blurt out a quick "no" without giving the serving invitation a fair hearing. "It sounds like work. No thanks. Been there, done that."

The automatic no is a perfect response to temptation and sin but an unsuitable knee-jerk reaction to many serving requests. We may with good reason turn down many invitations, but let's remain open to prayerfully considering and evaluating opportunities.

The whole idea of retirement as entitlement is worth talking about. We've planned for it, set money aside, now also qualify for Social Security, and feel like we're justifiably entitled to it. This is the honorable form of gratification, postponed not instant, and we've patiently waited a long time. Please, no bait and switch now!

At the micro level, we may attend to small specks of entitlement sawdust in the eyes of others, but the broader subject of our own entitlement to retirement is as American as the Splash Mountain log ride at Disneyland.

But what if we viewed the empty nest, our home, possessions, time, talents, and retirement as **belonging to God, not to us**—something He has entrusted to us as **stewards, not as owners**? Would we give them up if God asked us to? It's sure easy to cast blame on the rich young ruler Jesus encountered, but might we, too, walk away sorrowfully? It's hardly even comfortable to talk about.

We detest seeing a spirit of entitlement surface in others, but do we treat our own entitlements as off limits and fiercely defend them?

"I do what I want to do on my terms and timetable. If I want to coast, I coast. If I want to putter, I putter. If I want to play, I play. And woe be to any joy-robber who dares challenge my entitlements, these sacraments of retirement." This is a paraphrase, but we've all probably heard similar rants from both believers and non-Christians.

How does the Church walk through these American culture minefields? Or do we 'let sleeping dogs lie' and not even go there?

This can cut different ways. You may be a workaholic resisting retirement, and God may want you to slow down and step away from your employment to pursue something more significant, such as investing more time with your family. Or maybe you have adult kids in your home who need to grow up and move out—maybe God is telling you it's finally time to clear out your nest.

Or, going another direction, maybe you're vocationally retired, and God wants you to pursue an encore career.

Perhaps your empty nest is ready for foster parenting? Or you may want to volunteer for a week this summer as a camp grandparent with Royal Family Kids[41] (look it up!), or volunteer year-round with Samaritan Purse's Operation Christmas Child[42].

HALF TWO — DAY SEVEN

Up until now we've people-watched. Now we're probing a bit more deeply into Who/who is governing this great Land.

We certainly don't want to cast judgment, but it's often not too hard to discern by our conversations and actions, who (with a small 'w') might be calling the shots.

If we're going to refer to Jesus as Lord, let's get our marching orders from Him. That's the relationship that should define us, not some cultural stereotypes like 'Millennial', 'Baby Boomer', 'retiree', or 'empty nester'.

Infinitely Better

We may with good reasons love our generation, church, denomination, nation, and cultural heritage. But our grasp of kingdom breadth can weaken when we become too generational, too denominational, too national, or too culturally ingrained. It can narrow to, "My kingdom come, my will be done."

The kingdom of God transcends our generation, church,

denomination, political party, socio-economic background, community, county, state, nation, gender, language, life stage, personality type, even our favorite sports teams.

We can't pretend to know God's plan for you, but **His plans may be bigger and more unorthodox than you imagine**. We stress having a big heart open to hearing from God—and new possibilities, not limited or compartmentalized by societal norms.

Warning:
Some Shipment May Occur During Settling

While writing this chapter I received a note from Gary Geesey, a pastor in early retirement, letting me know that he and his wife Charlotte just said "Yes!" to an unexpected invitation to serve in Japan for a year, covering for a missionary returning to the States for a year of furlough. Very inspiring.

Recently Gary sent an email. "We have landed in Fukuoka and are getting settled in ... trying not to be too overwhelmed. We have great mentor missionaries to work with and believe incredible opportunities await us all as we partner together to see the church here flourish."

"We have been spurred on by the many encouraging words from family and friends ... so glad we said YES!"

And Charlotte later added, "We never dreamed we'd celebrate our 43rd trip around the sun together in Japan. God's plans and purposes are the BEST!"

Retirement Clock Tinkering

Many countries, including developed nations, do not firmly embed retirement in their culture. Work doesn't shut down at a certain or even general age. People may taper their work hours as they get older, but the idea of abruptly stopping work is foreign in many cultures. And even here in the United States, more people have started to question the wisdom of retirement as a universally expected norm.

We tend to forget how recently retirement systems became such an integral part of the American landscape. Social Security was enacted in 1935, and sixty-five was established as the normal retirement age. To give further context, life expectancy for those born that year was about sixty years. Those fortunate enough to reach sixty-five in 1935 could expect to live, on average, another twelve years.

One of the many major crises ahead for our nation is the exploding population of older retirees, particularly in comparison to the mainstream workforce. Between now and 2034, as Baby Boomers grow older, we can expect—daily—about ten thousand seventieth birthday parties.

For several years, as part of God's unexpected and miraculous provision, our strongest supporting church for *YES! Young Enough to Serve* was Trinity Christian Centre, a thriving church in Singapore. Reverend Dominic Yeo, a frequent US visitor, identified strongly with the mission of YES! and recognized that many Americans have not fully utilized the potential of older adults.

We've grown to appreciate that Asian cultures consistently demonstrate more respect for their elders, much more so than do their Western counterparts. It's embedded in their culture. 'Old' and 'older' in Singapore are compliments, not slander.

Because of this strong respect for older generations, family units tend to remain more closely knit together. Geographically, they position themselves much nearer each other, often with extended family members living in the same home. (They also have the advantage of much smaller landmass than the US!)

The Singaporean government even offers tax incentives to adult children choosing to live within a prescribed radius of their aging parents. This cross-generational concern and compassion reflects in the church as well, and Asian churches are typically blessed with stronger unity between generations.

Finally, Reverend Dominic pointed out that retirement in Singapore has comparatively a much softer emphasis. People continue working, as they are able, without expecting to retire at a certain age. Because of this, older Singaporean Christians also appear less tempted to drift into spiritual retirement. They know this is a prime season to influence others, not spiritually punching their final time card and closing up shop.

Re-Checking Numbers

We've heard many people say that retirement is unbiblical and that you won't find it in the Bible. Surprisingly, there is one verse in all of Scripture that mentions retirement,

Numbers 8:25. The Levites faced mandatory retirement at the young age of fifty. They also had to be at least twenty-five. So, the Levites and Sons operation had a twenty-five-year window of opportunity.

Bible scholars don't know for sure why God set up this mandatory retirement plan for the Levites. The physical demands of the position likely played a part, as well as need for a structure where leadership was consistently passed to subsequent generations. Although the Levites clearly had to relinquish their primary duties after fifty, they had permission to assist in other roles.

So, this passage represented a **shift in responsibility** rather than complete banishment from work or the temple. Many, no doubt, moved into a season of mentoring others, drawing from their rich heritage of serving as a Levite.

While this verse is Levite-specific and doesn't provide enough territory to build an intricate theology of retirement, we can't say that vocational retirement is unbiblical.

But we can say with Scriptural authority that there is no basis for **spiritual** retirement. Many stereotypes we associate with vocational retirement come today from marketing agents spinning a version of the American dream, without clear parallels in the Old or New Testament.

Open Our Hearts, Lord!

Claiming you don't work since you're retired should be about as ridiculous as saying a stay-at-home mom with toddlers doesn't work. Let's not assume work always comes with salaries and benefits. That thinking is much too narrow and limiting. Perhaps your retirement nest egg has paved the way for waiving the pay.

For the majority of us, employed or retired, life itself comes with lots of unpaid tasks that easily fall under the heading of work. Some work is just plain necessary to get on with the day, and some is more discretionary. Let's joyfully embrace both and use our freedom to serve others.

Let's move from, *"I'm retired, and it doesn't matter what I do"* to *"how I spend my days continues to matter ... a lot."* Our days are numbered, and how we collectively choose to live our final days and decades impacts every living generation, not just ourselves.

- ✓ So, we come face-to-face with this question for empty nesters and retirees: Is Jesus the Lord of our lives—after the kids are raised and after we've said goodbye to full-time employment?
- ✓ How do we capsize "whatever floats your boat" attitudes? Or should we?
- ✓ For those of us approaching traditional 'retirement years', let's ask the Lord if or when we should vocationally retire. How do we allow Him, not cultural norms, to shape how this season ahead can look? How can we further surrender our timetable to Him?
- ✓ If you've stepped out of circulation, how is God asking you to step back into the mix, using your gifts, talents, life experience, and wisdom? How will you respond?

Day 8. READY TO ROLL

Saying "Not Now" to Procrastination

And we urge you, brothers and sisters,
warn those who are idle and disruptive,
encourage the disheartened,
help the weak, be patient with everyone.
1 Thessalonians 5:14 (NIV)

WHAT MAKES US THINK we can go at things on our own for a stretch and then later get serious about tapping into God's agenda for our lives? Why don't we start with *"go and make disciples?"*

Think about how ludicrous these words sound, *"Not now, Lord."*

Imagine for a moment you and I are chefs at a restaurant owned and operated by the King of the Universe, and He directs us to primary ingredients He wants featured on the main course menu. We politely tell Him that we'll take His recommendations under advisement.

We're open to rolling out His Great Commission with some fanfare later, but we first have some more palatable appetizers in mind. We're not defiantly saying, *'No!'* It's just something we choose to postpone indefinitely. Meanwhile, ingredients for the King's main dish wilt on the counter.

For some new Christians, we see immediate, all-out abandonment. For others, we see an invitation for Christ to come into our kitchen, but we don't yet invite Him to open every drawer and cupboard—or enter other rooms of our home, for that matter.

"Don't go there, please. That pantry is a catch-all disaster, and I haven't had time yet to reorganize." But we fail to realize this Lord Jesus we've invited into our kitchen is more than willing to roll up His sleeves to help serve His dish and clean up other messes. He wants to replace our inadequacies with His strength. He is ready now, and we don't need to wait.

Let's turn for a moment to the fishermen Jesus called to be His disciples. Unworthy? Inadequate? Yes, yes. What if they had been unwilling in the present moment to lay down their nets to follow Him? After all, they were immersed in their professions and likely had mouths to feed and bills to pay. I'm sure some of them wrestled with the inconvenient timing of Jesus' invitation. It was an honor to be asked, but couldn't He just wait until fishing season was over? By staying with their nets, they too would have missed the boat.

Cat's in the Cradle

Sometimes our temporary put-offs remind us of Harry Chapin's *Cat's in the Cradle*[45] folk rock song. In it, the father sadly offers his son a litany of excuses for why he can't spend time with him at that moment, followed by unfulfilled future promises. And in the end, the son unhappily becomes just like his father.

In our skit adaptation below, our Father asks, "When are you going to serve Me?" *We, too, don't know when, but we'll have a good time then.*

It alternates with female and male (*italicized*) responses, and the bold headings are read in unison:

No, we're *too young* to serve!

- 5: No, I just started kindergarten!

- *10: No, I don't know enough yet. Come on, I'm only in fourth grade! I think there are child labor laws that make this sort of thing illegal.*

- 15: No, I don't have my driver's license.

- *17: No, I'm not eighteen yet. Somebody said I couldn't serve my country until I turn 18. Last I checked, our address is still in the USA, right?*

- 21: No, I'm still in college. I haven't graduated yet. Maybe when these studies are behind me, I'll be able to devote some time to serving.

No, we're just *too busy* to serve!

- *23: No, I need to find a job.*

- 24: No, I'm working full-time, plus a lot of overtime, and I get only two weeks vacation. Maybe when those student loans are paid off and vacation expands to three weeks, I might be able to give a day or two.

- *25: No, we're engaged. We need to focus on our relationship right now.*

• 26: No, we just got married, and we're busy saving for our first home.

• *27: No, we just got our first home, but it's a fix-me-upper. That's just another way of saying it's all **up** to **me** to **fix** it!*

• 28: No, we're expecting our first child. We're taking parenting and prenatal care classes. We're also getting the nursery ready.

• *30: No, we have two kids under two. Need we say more?*

• 32: No, we have three kids under four. Sorry, we're just not in a position to help right now.

• *36: No, our kids are all involved in sports. As it is, we have to split up as a couple to make it to all their games.*

• 40: No, we're away on weekends. Did we tell you about our boat?

• *43: No, we're pretty tied up now with some investment properties.*

• 45: No, our kids are getting ready for college, and we have to work extra hours to pay for their education. We're almost at the empty nest stage … maybe then.

No, we *need a break*! We've just entered the empty nest.

• *52: No, this is the first time we've had the joy of being together as a couple without having to think every minute about our kids. It's a little bit like our second honeymoon. We're dating again … now is just not the time to commit to serving.*

• 54: No, give us some time. We have a lot of delayed gratification items on our bucket list that we can finally get to … not to mention the "honey do" list.

- *56: No, one of our kids just moved back.*

- 57: No, our daughter's wedding is coming up.

- *59: No, maybe when our "boomerang" child leaves home, we'll be ready to serve.*

- 60: No, did I mention that we now have grandchildren? If I have any extra energy, that's where it's going.

- *62: No, we're kind of focused on saving and preparing for retirement right now. Maybe when we actually retire we can think about serving.*

No, we're *retired*!

- 65: No, we've been slaves to our jobs for so many years. Now we're finally our own bosses. We can stay up late and sleep in as late as we want. This is our time to relax and enjoy life.

- *67: No, you certainly don't expect us to tie ourselves down now with a serving commitment, do you?*

- 69: No, we really want to spend some time traveling and seeing the world, and of course, we both want to work on our golf game.

- *71: No, maybe when our frequent flyer miles are used up, we'll think about serving.*

No, come to think of it, we're *too old* to serve!

- 74: No, let the younger people do it.

- *76: Yeah, they're the ones with all the energy!*

What Makes Them Tick?

Early on, working with adults over fifty, we engaged in some *reverse engineering* conversations with adults serving Christ fervently in their later years. By then, some of these *full-throttle* Christians had serious mobility issues and were no longer able to actively participate in many church activities. But they were still active in telling their stories — through writing, blogging, phone and in-person conversations — spreading the gospel to any and all they met.

When did their light bulbs go on? What made them different from more complacent Christians, who seemed to lose power at the breaker switch? We encourage you to initiate similar conversations with older adults in your church whose present exemplary lives are worth emulating.

Probe their history as followers of Christ. Get into who, what, when, why, where, and how. When did you become a Christian? What led up to that? Who was the first person you led to Christ? Were there times of significant faith surges forward? How about times when you weren't firing on all cylinders? What keeps you from spiritually retiring? Favorite Scripture verses?

For most of those we interviewed, this passionate fire had been lit much earlier in life. Then when they reached the ripe ages of fifty, sixty, or seventy, there was little thought of slowing down and certainly no thought of quitting. Yes, some had reduced physical stamina, but they continued to ask the

Lord for His help and re-direction in making an impact for Him.

One gentleman I interviewed shared that when he committed his life to Christ at the age of eight, he knew immediately that God had called him to be a soul winner. He still lives out this revelation in his ninth decade.

But what about those who didn't seem to get a similar revelation at the time of conversion? We know many Christians who just seem personally content to be on a path to heaven, disciples but not disciple-makers. Is there hope for the more introverted, non-multipliers among us?

Some interviewees pointed to a single aha moment occurring after the time they initially put their trust in Christ. Some shared testimonies of how *"Jesus was my Savior but then became my Lord."* Others referred to a special encounter with the Holy Spirit, the third person of the Trinity.

For some, light bulbs grew progressively brighter, and for others, a series of moments and life experiences propelled them to shine more brightly—along with some admitted seasons of setback when their dimmable light switch had inched closer to the 'off' position.

Commission Omission

The gospel is not suffering in America because of a shortage of building space or amenities such as 'coffee coves'. Plain and simple, we have a shortage of disciple-makers.

For several years, Judy and I have taught at the Legacy

Conference at Mount Hermon Christian Conference Center[44]. Interestingly, when we earlier included *"Making Disciples"* in our workshop title, the attendance was much lower. Many felt intimidated to walk into the room. Some tiptoed in, admitting that the workshop title conjured up feelings of both fear and guilt, and these were mature Christians interested in leaving a meaningful legacy.

Why do we sheepishly skirt around the Great Commission from the lips of Jesus, who instructed us to go and make disciples? If we truly believe this Half Two of our lives belongs to Him, can we trust Him to set our agenda and priority? Why do we call Him 'Lord' while letting His Great Commission become irrelevant, minor, deferred, conveniently outside our wheelhouse, or just a nagging source of guilt?

If my life is half His and half mine, I'll let my fear and guilt stand in the way of His commission. I'll find enough wiggle room to justify my noncompliance:

- "It's not my calling."
- "I don't have the gift of evangelism."
- "My job is to work quietly in the background and support others who have this special calling."
- "This is a season of life when it's perfectly okay to say 'No' and feel good about it."

Let's Do This!

We need to do a better job setting people up for success in this important calling! Personally and collectively, we need to be open to course corrections, even in Half Two when life patterns may seem cemented and unlikely to change.

Paul gave the younger Timothy and Titus full authority to dispense encouragement and correction. They likely didn't need his authority to encourage, but neither did Paul want them correcting without a base of encouragement. We need healthy portions of both.

Even here I'm tiptoeing with the most tactful word I can find, settling on 'correction'. Other translations refer to their authority to encourage and *rebuke, refute,* or *reprove.*

We know the adage, "You catch more flies with honey than you do with vinegar" and the question, "Is the glass half empty or half full?" Like the much-maligned participation trophies awarded to Millennials, truth gets camouflaged when we dispense only the honey or half-full message.

We can appreciate Paul's sequence, starting with encouragement first, but let's not stop there. After our half-full high fives, maybe we need to ask, "Could there be a correlation between empty seats in the back of our cars and empty pews in the front of our churches?"

According to a 2016 Barna study[45], almost half (46 percent) of American churchgoers attend a church of one hundred or fewer members. We can appreciate the intimacy of smaller churches, but the number of empty seats or vacant pews is disturbing. We've seen them on our travels throughout the United States, inching closer to the hollow European cathedrals.

Jesus prescribes a primary way we can spread His love

and build His kingdom—by making disciples. Let's not settle for an endless buffet of self-concocted appetizers that prolong our procrastination and kill our appetite for the main course. We don't know how much more time we have to make a difference in the lives of others.

We are not alone in our fears. Many other mature Christians share the same hesitation and feelings of inadequacy. The distance we've traveled with Christ compounds the shame, another trick the enemy uses to cause discouragement and retreat. **Let's step outside our comfort zones *now*, and let the testimony of what follows encourage others to do the same.**

In the United States, the 'evangelical' label has sadly become a noun and political voting block. We're good at voting, but we've neglected the root verb form, *"to evangelize."*

Over eighty percent of American Christians admit that they have never personally led someone into a relationship with Christ. If we're part of the 80+ percent, we might find a measure of comfort in this sobering statistic … misery does love company. But what can we do—individually and corporately—to help move professing Christians outside this guilt-plagued cohort? We have to do better.

Again, Satan wants us to beat ourselves up and go to our graves wishing we had only done more—or simply die content in knowing we were part of the silent, sterile majority.

We find too many adults over fifty who are spiritually retired, generationally separated, and willfully out of Commission. As in the Garden, we hear a gentle voice saying there's nothing wrong with a non-viral lifestyle of leisure and segregation, especially in our later years. It's our own special Tree, and we deserve to eat from it.

Half Two — Day Eight

Today we traveled to a beach community where some inhabitants seem blissfully devoted to simple pleasures like watching the waves roll in and out—and collecting seashells. They've extended what was once occasional weekend leisure into weeks, months, years, and decades of carefree living.

Part of us envies these sun-drenched American dreamers living the 'good life', and the other part knows they may be missing out on a 'better life'. Have to make it better! How will we do it?

Don't Sell Yourself Short

Not to justify our timidity or injured self-esteem, it's helpful to acknowledge that people who come to faith in Christ have often had about seven positive touch-points along the way. The number, labels, and sequence of these positive touch-points will vary, but you may have helped an unbeliever:

- Build initial awareness of the Christian faith,
- Grow in his/her trust and openness to God,
- Know an authentic Christian of integrity,

- See firsthand the benefits of following Christ,
- Diminish their resistance to faith,
- Remove fear,
- Reduce negative Christian stereotypes,
- Appreciate Scripture,
- Observe answered prayer,
- Walk away from negative influences,
- Make friends with other Christians,
- Increase their understanding of Jesus, Savior,
- Step inside a church for the first time,
- Know the pathway to salvation,
- Open the door to the Holy Spirit's gentle prodding.

You may have been "touch numbers" two and six in many lives but may not yet have experienced touch seven, actually leading someone into relationship with Christ. Without necessarily knowing it, you may have been a powerful witness preparing someone's heart to receive Christ, or a strong discipling force in the life of a new Christian.

While it's likely that we may have missed some opportune moments along the way to *"seal the deal,"* let's recognize that making disciples is broader than making converts or leading someone in the sinner's prayer[46].

Think about it. Who helped disciple you in your walk with Christ? Chances are, you can point to many who discipled you, not just one person. As the Apostle Paul shared, *I planted the seed in your hearts, and Apollos watered it, but it was God who made it grow.* 1 Corinthians 3:6 (NLT)

Nothing But the Blessed

Why then do we choose procrastination over becoming proactive in the disciple-making arena? It could be self-centeredness. And it's usually sprinkled with elements of fear, both rational and irrational—with an accompanying unwillingness to confront our fears.

With retirement from secular jobs, we also commonly see diminished relationships with non-Christians. Our lives can become overly saturated with those of like-minded faith, and intentional contact and natural relationships with others can become less common.

Shifts in technology enable shopping via Amazon, banking online and at ATM's, self-pumping gas, and even self-service checkout at grocery and other retail stores. They've made it easy for us to avoid face-to-face human interaction and incrementally build our cocoons.

Along with many secular and some faith-based nonprofits, YES! currently partners with *Generation to Generation*[47], an Encore.org affiliate, mobilizing adults 50+ to help young people thrive. We encourage you to scour their generationtogeneration.org website for additional intergenerational, bridge-building ideas both inside and outside your church walls.

It may seem paradoxical, referring you to often non-proselytizing environments, in the context of our disciple-making discussion. We are called to be both salt and light in this world. Your participation and presence can make a life-changing difference in people you serve and in those serving alongside you—even when you're perhaps not allowed to share your faith as openly and directly as you can with Christian-based outreaches.

Salt compliments and preserves, and light is all about contrast. Your light is most valuable in dark but open places, not in direct sunlight always surrounded by other Christians but also not hidden *under a bushel*. Jesus wants our light shining from a lampstand, for all in darkness to see.

Fortunately, there are some amazing resources to guide believers who want to help new Christians in their early walks with Christ. The Gospel of John is a great book to study with a seeker or new believer. Rather than presenting an incomplete list of other resources here, I encourage you to Google "resources for making disciples" or ask your pastor for recommendations.[48]

When opportunities surface, don't decline these God-ordained mentoring invitations because of your lack of experience or insecurity. Avail yourself of the resources available, and take the plunge. Learn together with your apprentice.

Yes, there will always be people more qualified to whom you could refer others, but we've all been called to make disciples. It's not meant to be an elite activity. Remember, focus on being warm and authentic with whomever God is calling you to disciple. And pray fervently that He will guide you as your share. Bring others alongside you to help.

We love the tagline of the ministry of ServeNow[49]: **"Serve Now, Procrastinate Later."**

Beyond Our Own Surf and Turf

We've been coddled long enough with a misplaced *'start in your comfort zone'* theology. It sounds perfectly logical to start in our comfort zone and then eventually move the pegs of our tent outward as our confidence builds. The truth is, confidence within our comfort zone doesn't always give us courage to leave what's comfortable—it may build attachment.

Many of us spend our lives carefully navigating around things we deem uncomfortable. It's time to plow through some of the fears and obstacles we've been avoiding. Public speaking was formerly one such fear for me. Writing my first book is another.

We've seen many Half Two programs that started more than a decade ago with a strong entertainment emphasis, with plans that they'd eventually move into a stronger serving and disciple-making mode, after building critical mass and momentum. But here they are, more than a decade later, still confined to a fairly closed circuit of *fun, food, and fellowship*, still catering to the hometown crowd's more timid wishes.

Can God use this strategy? By all means. He loves to meet people where they are. Jesus met people at their point of need, but the connecting points for many of these relationships were also their serving potential:

- The woman at the well, asking her for water.
- The disciples and their potential to become fishers of men.
- Even the rich young ruler and his potential to give and impact the poor.

We're looking for clarion calls to serve. After almost gluttonous intakes of Bible studies, hymn sings, and potlucks, do our personal and church calendars reflect our desire for what's most comfortable—or engagement with God's wisdom, calling, courage, and supernatural/Scriptural direction?

As leaders working with people approaching the end of life, we must be careful where we start. Because the reality is, our tenure may be short, and we may end where we start. Start with a kingdom perspective, prayer, servant's heart, and a commitment to fulfill the Great Commission together. Today. If these become *eventual* goals, you or at least some of those you lead may never get there.

Must following God be uncomfortable? No. But even if you find yourself both fruitful and comfortable in your 'sweet spot', it's always good to accept new challenges. While *"no pain, no gain"* isn't necessarily Scriptural, we want to practice faith in arenas where God simply has to show up.

As a proof text for starting in our familiarity zone, we might point to Jesus' parting instructions to His disciples. *But you will receive power when the Holy Spirit comes on you; and you will be my witnesses **in Jerusalem, and in all Judea and Samaria, and to the ends of the earth.*** Acts 1:8 (NIV)

We hear Jerusalem commonly used as a metaphor to

represent starting in our hometown, where we're most comfortable, and then branching out into broader geographic circles. Jerusalem was familiar territory but not the disciples' hometown. They were Galileans. Jesus had earlier directed them away from the Sea of Galilee to the city of Jerusalem, likely because it was a strategic center of world commerce.

Whatever the reason, it's important to note that Jesus gave the directions. He didn't put it to a vote, or leave it up to the disciples based on their own personal preferences or *Taylor-Johnson Temperament Analysis*[50]. If so, they would likely have chosen to stay one chapter back in John 21, pursuing another miraculous catch on the shores of the Sea of Galilee.

Left to their own devices, fishing was a very logical, natural, post-resurrection, fallback plan. But, in this pivotal moment in Church history, Jesus wanted them to take huge steps forward and to bloom where they weren't planted.

- The disciples weren't city folk. Jesus said go to Jerusalem.
- They were outdoorsmen. They were directed inside to an upper room.
- They were active, mobile, and impetuous. Jesus said wait there for the Holy Spirit.

Acts 2 / Half 2

The disciples' attachment to their fishing nets never again surfaces in the New Testament, after the John 21 passage. We shouldn't make too much of the silence, but it does appear that carrying out God's will from that point forward had little to do with the disciples' personal predispositions. More than ever, they truly became fishers of men, empowered by the Holy Spirit, and they surrendered to God's agenda, not their own.

Certainly, we're not ruling out fishing or your favorite hobby—unless God is asking you to give up something standing in the way of your obedience to Him. As I saw one day in a gift shop, *"Give a man a fish, and you've fed him for a day. Teach a man to fish, and he'll sit in a boat drinking beer with his buddies all day."*

God may actually want you to creatively use your favorite hobby for His kingdom purposes. How about offering to take that fourth grade boy whose dad committed suicide last year to the driving range? That upcoming, five-mile hike you've planned with your husband or friend? Invite some junior high girls to join you.

Perhaps we're prone to give personal preference too much reverence. Scripture is clear from Acts 2 forward that the disciples didn't start in their comfort zone, and they undeniably didn't end there.

Typical questions in American culture begin with: "Where do YOU see YOURSELF in five years? What are YOUR big, audacious goals? What do YOU want to do in YOUR retirement? What's on YOUR bucket list? And second half adult leaders ask their followers, *"What's YOUR pleasure? What fun things do YOU retirees want to do as a group?"*

These reasonable pathways uncover some personal

passions and creative understanding of how God has wired us. And let's remember to enjoy the journey. Jesus said, "My yoke is easy. My burden is light." But this doesn't mean we look to hitch our wagons to whatever we perceive to be easy and light. We start with His yoke, His burden.

Our responses can shed light on how much pleasing God factors into our plans. Hopefully, our answers to these common, me-centered questions tie quickly to God's continued calling and agenda in our lives. Not our will, but His be done.

Quoting D.L. Moody, "Our greatest fear should not be of failure, but of succeeding at something that doesn't really matter."[51]

We can't make His FIRSTS eventual goals, subplots or afterthoughts. Let's make His firsts our firsts. Let's go and make disciples now, procrastinate later. This is ground zero, and we have a life of adventure ahead, potentially more fruitful than we ever dreamed.

✓ In the next ten minutes, what can you do to help create movement outside one of your comfort zones? What will help motivate you to act?

✓ Okay, set your timer for ten minutes. Instead of only discussing hypothetically what you could do, actually spend the next ten minutes doing it. Sometimes, getting started is half the battle.

Day 9. RESORT ACCOMMODATIONS

Prayer as Our First Resort

Look to the LORD and his strength; seek his face always.
1 Chronicles 16:11 (NIV)

"WELL, IF YOU CAN'T SERVE, YOU CAN *AT LEAST* PRAY." Did we really just say that?

As we started YES!, we were pretty zealous in the serving project, missions trip, and outreach arenas, getting adults over fifty off their duffs and into some significant serving opportunities. And that passion continues as our geographic scope expands. Now, however, rather than create a whole new smorgasbord of serving opportunities directly through YES!, we've placed a stronger emphasis on serving through their local churches.

While we try to avoid projects requiring significant physical prowess, many of our outreaches have been understandably beyond the physical capacity of our frail elderly. Some adults have participated by dropping off cookies for work teams or showing up just to provide

153

encouragement. Yet many lack the strength even to make an appearance at our serving sites.

Some of our less physically capable adults have apologized for being able *only to pray for us* and not physically share in the workload. While we acknowledge that these projects need physical effort, warning bells started going off. We became uncomfortable attaching an apologetic tone to prayer.

Since when did prayer take a back seat to serving? Since when was prayer not in itself a powerful, compassionate act of obedience and service? **Real servants pray. Prayer is powerful. There's no small nor wasted prayer.**

We felt convicted. Prayer needed to move to the forefront of what we were doing. While some team members find more time to pray than others, we all need to be on our knees before God. And we need to practice an ongoing form of prayer that continues after we get up. As the Apostle Paul instructs, *pray without ceasing.*

We recently changed our YES! mission statement, moving prayer ahead of serving: *"With help from all generations, YES! helps inspire adults over fifty to become more intentional in **praying**, serving, and making disciples."*

Warriors in Prayer

Most of us know people who are absolutely tenacious in prayer. We salute them as prayer warriors, our *go to* intercessors.

Just as Judy and I bear the official title of "missionaries" and believe all Christians share in that same calling, we know God calls all of us to become more deliberate, consistent, and tenacious in our prayer lives. Yes, there will still be people we tend to single out as having special gifts and calling related to prayer, but we can all grow in our prayer lives—even as the aging process hammers our physical bodies.

We love the movie, **War Room**. What a great picture of an older adult woman grasping the power of prayer. If you have not yet seen this movie, consider a short reading break to watch the trailer linked in the footnotes.[52]

Judy was inspired to the point that she converted our daughter's bedroom into her favorite closet of prayer, and she faithfully adds both prayer needs and answers to her prayer board.

HALF TWO — DAY NINE

Wow, now we're getting somewhere deep, far beyond just sightseeing from a distance. Today we were invited into the home of an older prayer warrior, who is actually partnering with God to change the world from her prayer closet. Very motivating and life-changing! Someone who truly believes in and practices the power of prayer!

Beyond Dutiful

We know that true prayer is not just a formal exercise that God wants us to engage in by rote, like a dutiful form of spiritual calisthenics. Yes, it is a wonderful discipline with huge personal dividends, but prayer is so much bigger than us. It represents conversation with the King of Kings and Lord of Lords. It takes us into realms of possibility and perspective not found on a human level. We can travel without a traffic jam, jump continents, and touch heaven.

We not only talk with God about things already on our heart or on our prayer list. He can lead the conversation and the burden of our heart in new directions. He'll bring people, needs, and concerns to mind that we were not consciously thinking about earlier.

Most of us can relate to E.B. White's daybreak travail, "Every morning when I wake up, I am torn between the twin desires to reform the world and to enjoy the world, and it makes it hard to plan the day."[53]

Through prayer, God can help us sort out some of these hard daily choices. Ideally, we can learn to enjoy reforming the world. I sense that Mother Teresa enjoyed her work.

As we actively listen, God can help blaze new trails, lead us into new and stronger relationships, and help us foster more deliberate serving and disciple-making opportunities. He can build our confidence and give us specific words and tasks to help shape our minutes, hours, and days.

"I was praying this morning, and God brought you to my mind." You've hopefully heard this from others many times. How great to know Christians who faithfully set aside time to pray, and what a blessing to know that God cares about us in such a personal way! We can do the same in our verbal or written conversation with others, as He directs. It's a rich way to

allow God to begin directing more of our thoughts, actions, agendas, and relationships—using us to touch the lives of others.

I've also learned over the years to pray immediately with or for someone with an expressed need. It's not always possible or practical, but too often we settle for promising to keep someone in our thoughts and prayers, rather than interceding right on the spot, in person or over the phone. Isn't it uplifting to hear someone pray in a heartfelt, authentic, and expectant way? The presence of God becomes more real. He is right there with us.

And, of course, if we promise to pray in the future, let's keep our promise and do just that. If you're prone to forget, jot down the prayer request as soon as you can, pray consistently and then follow up.

Remember, prayer requires a pray-er.

God Answers

Best of all, God answers prayer. Not always in the exact way we think He will—sometimes wildly exceeding our finite imaginations, sometimes painfully testing our finite understanding.

I feel inadequate even to write this chapter on prayer because I so often fail to enter God's throne room and interact in an honest, personal way with our Redeemer. But it's also okay to be a 63-year-old apprentice, learning from God and others to move more consistently in this realm, allowing Him to fight our battles.

Judy and I have a special friendship and mentoring relationship with Brian and Leona, a young couple from our church. They approached us a couple years ago and affirmed how we had raised our four kids. At the early stages of raising their family, they wanted an ongoing relationship, conversation, and prayer with a more seasoned Christian couple, and we were thrilled to be asked. We've met faithfully for a meal almost every month, either at our home or theirs—a very rich opportunity.

Consider a prayer friendship with another person or couple. It usually starts with more casual friendship, and it takes a courageous someone to break the ice. As older adults, we need to project a sincere love and appreciation for younger generations and show an openness to serve by putting ourselves in position to be asked.

It certainly doesn't have to start with the questions, "Will you mentor me?" Or, "will you be my prayer partner?" But on rare occasions when this does occur, be ready to say, "Yes!"—even if you might feel a personal sense of inadequacy.

In sharing life with Brian and Leona, we've found plenty of needs to pray about together. One evening they said they needed to move out of their condo and that their early search for a new residence was extremely discouraging for their family of three. They contemplated moving out of state to find more affordable rent.

We shared briefly from our own experience how God has been so faithful to provide miracle housing when we asked

Him for it. It was fun to tell a couple of our miracle stories, and we encouraged them to pray for a miracle so that they could stay in Scotts Valley, as they wanted to do.

As we prayed together, God dropped names of a couple into my heart; they owned a vacant duplex in Scotts Valley. It needed work, but we thought perhaps Brian and Leona might move into one unit and help the older owners rehabilitate the other unit in exchange for reduced rent.

The next day I met with the duplex owners, and they were receptive to meeting Brian and Leona and showing them the property. At first it looked like the miracle might progress exactly as we had prayed and envisioned, but then the owners decided not to rent to our younger friends—resisting the idea of again becoming landlords. Our hearts sank, but we still prayed for a miracle, knowing that God might lead our friends to some other property.

A couple of weeks later, we received another call requesting prayer. Brian and Leona were getting ready to meet with a real estate loan agent to see if they might qualify for a home loan. Based on their prior experience, it seemed like a long shot, but we agreed to pray.

Another two weeks later they were over for dinner, excitedly sharing the news that their loan application had been approved, and their subsequent offer to purchase **the duplex** was accepted!

After dinner and after expressing heartfelt praise to the Lord, we gladly let them use our home office to scan final documents to close the deal. Our hearts were full, rejoicing over God's provision.

We've seen God come through so many times, but it never gets old. God is faithful, yet it never ceases to blow us away. If God places it on your heart to pray for a miracle, we encourage you to trust and persevere. He is more than able to do above what our finite minds can ask or think.

Still, miracles may also come with a lot of hard work. Brian and Leona then faced a challenging summer to ready the other half of their duplex for renters. Their many friends and family members stepped in to help complete the remodel. By summer's end, the Lord blessed them with delightful renters, and before winter ended, they welcomed their second child.

Beyond God's miraculous provision, we once again rejoiced in the value of having both younger and older friends. Because we had relationships with both the older and younger couples, we could pray for them and watch as God enabled solutions for the needs of each.

To God be the glory! He's the author and finisher of our faith! And He wants us to pass on our faith generationally.

✓ We encourage you to befriend an older or younger individual/couple with whom you can share life, share needs and pray together. We who are older realize that God has entrusted us with a storied lifetime to help illustrate His faithful provision. What are some of your favorite stories? Share them, and then together in prayer, trust God for new stories of His tender and miraculous care.

✓ With whom might you engage as new friendship partners?

DESTINATION III.

Half Two—
Make It COUNT!

Onward,
FOREWORD to Destination III

Half Two—*Make It COUNT!*

Dr. Amy Hanson

ALMOST THIRTY YEARS AGO, God began stirring in me a desire to help older adults live out their lives with meaning and purpose. I believed then what I believe with even more fervor today: Everyone is valuable to God, and we can all make our lives count for eternity.

The hard part is that so many of us get pulled into the world's view of the second-half of life. We buy into the myths that "we've done our time and paid our dues" and "we should let others do it now." Or we feel marginalized by family, friends and even the church. We may think that this is a time to focus solely on leisure and personal pursuits.

But God's Word says something entirely different:

> *The righteous will flourish like a palm tree, they will grow like a cedar of Lebanon; planted in the house of the Lord, they will flourish in the courts of our God. They will still bear fruit in old*

age, they will stay fresh and green, proclaiming, "The Lord is upright; He is my Rock, and there is no wickedness in Him. Psalm 92: 12-15 (NIV)

Staying fresh and green has nothing to do with our physical bodies but has everything to do with having a willing and surrendered heart—that desires to make a difference for the Kingdom of God. This might include mission trips, second careers and even starting new ministries, but 'making it count' goes beyond that.

Making it count is:

The empty-nest couple who upon donating their used furniture to a ministry for women getting out of prison, offer to deliver it to her. The friendship they strike up prompts the young woman to invite this couple to her wedding at the courthouse, where the only four people in attendance are the empty-nesters and the bride and groom!

Making it count is:

The group of retired men who weekly serve together in the local homeless mission sharing encouragement and hope.

Making it count is:

The sixty-something woman who meets with the younger woman—and listens and mentors her regarding a struggling marriage—and then sends encouraging texts and prayers throughout the week.

Half Two—Make It COUNT is a bold call to all of us, to push beyond our comfort zones and broaden our view of what the second-half of life can be.

It's a challenge to the retired and the still working; the paid pastor and the lay-leader; the Christ follower and the unconnected; the young and the old. So read on with anticipation and expectation, and see what God will do.

Amy Hanson, Ph.D.
amyhanson.org
Author, *Baby Boomers and Beyond: Tapping the Ministry Talents and Passions of Adults over 50*

DESTINATION III. OVERVIEW

Half Two—*Make It COUNT!*

For you have been called to live in freedom, my brothers and sisters.
But don't use your freedom to satisfy your sinful nature.
Instead, use your freedom to serve one another in love.
Galatians 5:13 (NLT)

IT CAN BE TRICKY IN AMERICAN CULTURE to tie any inference of measurement to life's second half. Isn't this a season when we toss our cares to the wind and stop counting?

We may prefer to stop counting birthdays that call attention to our advancing years, or quit punching time clocks that meticulously measure and monitor workdays, hours, and minutes.

Still, most of us want our lives to **count** in the lives of others. Freedom and purpose are not mutually exclusive. We can allow both to co-exist and reign.

A book written by twin teenage brothers, Alex and Brett Harris, intrigued us. They wrote ***Do Hard Things***[54] as a teenage rebellion against low expectations. Teenagers are typically still years away from their career entry points, and societal expectations for their 'doing' potential can be quite low.

Similarly, adults on the other side of their career can also experience the dull ache of low expectations. Unfortunately, even within Christian circles, the expectation bar related to doing/serving can often be set embarrassingly low.

As one retired engineer lamented, "My primary church volunteer assignment is to arrange cookies on plates for snacks during the midweek boys' program." We can imagine those cookies were precisely arranged, but the church had not yet tapped into other abilities that he would willingly share.

In the book, *Prime Time: How Baby Boomers Will Revolutionize Retirement and Transform America*[55], author Marc Freedman tells a sad tale about Thea Glass, MD, who retired in Palm Beach, Florida, following a distinguished, four-decade career in medicine. She approached the local hospital with an enticing offer: "Put me to work in a way that makes use of my experience, capacities and passion for medicine, and you can have my services free of charge."

Marc continues, "After some consideration, the hospital informed the recent medical school department chair that they were pleased to offer her a new volunteer position … refilling water pitchers."

Were these retired professionals above the tasks of arranging cookies or refilling water pitchers? No. But they were both ready to offer far more. For these willing volunteers, the expectation bar was set way too low, squandering potential.

Not Over Until the Fat Lady Sings

Think about the second half excitement that can happen in sports. Even when our team faces a huge deficit at halftime, we still hope that we're about to witness one of the greatest comebacks in sports history.

However, we're sometimes prone to give up early and rely too heavily on first half performance as a predictor of Half Two outcome.

As parents, we were very excited about the Scotts Valley High School Falcon's very first varsity football league game. It was a new school, so new that it had not yet added a senior class, and our middle son Andrew was their first quarterback. Our hopes were sky high going into this inaugural game.

But the opposing school held our team scoreless in the first half, and we trailed 27-0. It was very disheartening, and our earlier optimism seemed almost embarrassing.

You probably sense where this story is going, but our associate pastor Chris didn't have a clue. In conversation with our lead pastor Jason later that Saturday, he confessed that he left the game at halftime. "So, you didn't see the second half?" Jason asked. "No, I had enough. I felt so bad for our guys," Chris replied.

"You left before the second half?" Jason repeated with a grin.

Well, as you may suspect, the second half completely reversed the first. Our guys came back in miraculous fashion and won the game, 28-27. Chris kicked himself for walking away early and giving up on the Falcons. He missed a thrilling comeback and unforgettable finish.

But it's not just Chris. We are all guilty at times of walking away from Half Two potential, in its various forms.

Serving in this area of ministry, you'd think I'd know better. One June evening a few years ago as I flipped through TV channels, I saw that the San Francisco Giants led the Houston Astros 10-0 after five innings. This game had a foregone conclusion; I was not about to waste my time watching it. I even told Judy that I felt sorry for the fans sitting through the remaining four innings. "There is no way they will come back," I said with smug authority.

I was right. Houston didn't mount a comeback. Not surprisingly, the game ended with that same fifth-inning score, a 10-0 blowout.

What I failed to observe, though, by changing channels so quickly, was that the Giants' pitcher Matt Cain had a perfect game going. Those fans, whom I pitied earlier, were fortunate enough to witness the first perfect game ever in the Giants' franchise, the 22nd perfect game in Major League Baseball history. Cain also tied Sandy Koufax's record for the most strikeouts in a perfect game, 14. Better than a no-hitter, a perfect game means no opposing team member reached first base.

And I, a strong advocate for Half Two potential, missed out on the live drama of those last four innings. I was so right about the outcome—and completely wrong.

And the pity I was feeling for those fans? Ironically, it's

the same kind of "bless your heart" pity Judy and I sometimes sense from people when they hear we're working with older adults. They, too, haven't yet reached first base in grasping how exciting Half Two ministry can be.

Snuffed Potential

Many Half Two church programs do their best to minister to the frail elderly, carefully accommodating a wide range of disabilities. At the same time, though, our one-size-fits-all programs often fail to capitalize on the wider range of abilities possessed by adults over fifty. The newsletter and sign on the door may say "50+", but activities suggest a target audience well over 70.

Field trips, potlucks, hymn sings, and cruises find their way to the top of the agenda, while missions trips, friendship partners, construction teams, coaching, mentoring, RV ministry [56], foster grandparenting [57], and other serving opportunities too often fall by the wayside.

Programs designed for a broad age spectrum have their limitations. Imagine trying to reach everyone under fifty with a singular program. We fervently hope to see adults on the plus side of fifty more fully recognizing and using the various shapes of potential still within their grasps. While some potential fades over time, other potentialities may still surge.

We don't suggest you divide your 50+ adults into two groups, such as 50-70 and 70+. We do encourage you to offer a range of ministry opportunities with varying degrees of challenge, and let your people self-select based on their own functional capacities. Chronological and functional ages are often far from being the same. You may have adults in their fifties who can't keep pace with certain adults in their eighties.

Is your church moving people in a vibrant, counter-cultural direction? Or does your church support, consciously or not, the low expectations of our culture?

Do we bring all our activities down to the lowest common denominator of physical ability, quietly hoping Boomers and Gen Xers will set aside their physical strength, passion, gifts, and current realities in favor of a tamer and gentler pursuit of leisure and fellowship?

Are we nurturing a Palm Sunday, *what's-in-it-for-me* sort of faith? We wave our palm branches today because what's happening right now fits with our cultural understanding of how perfectly life should play out for people of faith. Throw in a scourging, death sentence, cross, and tomb—and we're out of here.

Ward Tanneberg shares from experience that "the second half of life is neither automatically wonderful nor inherently depressing."

As I read the New Testament, I have a hard time envisioning some of our late-life biblical heroes finding themselves at home in some of our cozy, sedate church cultures. Some were too busy getting shipwrecked and tortured in prison—and still found time to write encouraging letters to others. Incidentally, those letters from two thousand years ago have a readership today greater than any blogs and Facebook posts—and trump any Tweets!

Will I feel and think differently when I'm in my seventies and eighties? Very likely so (assuming I'm still around), but I hope I will still nudge those in every decade of life to live a life **in the present** worthy of genuine respect, not simply dutiful respect stemming from our growing tally of trips around the sun.

Let's pursue these years with hearts intent on making Half Two count. And let's fix our eyes on Jesus, who moved counter to contemporary religious culture and showed us a better way.

Day 10. SECOND LANGUAGE

Who Are Your *Sticky Faith* Five?

Even in old age they will still produce fruit;
they will remain vital and green.
Psalm 92:14 (NLT)

TENACIOUS IN LOOKING AT SUSTAINED FAITH BEYOND HIGH SCHOOL and in emerging adult years, the Fuller Youth Institute in Pasadena, California, has completed significant research relevant to our discussion.

Kara Powell and her colleagues wrote the books *Sticky Faith*[58] and, more recently, *Growing Young*[59]. They are deeply concerned about the spiritual fallout that happens with many late adolescents and emerging adults who earlier seemed committed to Christ for a lifetime.

The most pronounced point of abandoned faith occurs as students graduate from high school and simultaneously graduate from their youth group, church, and their faith. Many find their way to secular colleges and universities where they often hear that their faith is a narrow, antiquated,

177

and discardable crutch from their earlier adolescent years.

Many other students, however, do not succumb to this slippery, *Teflon-coated* faith. One golden thread of research caught our attention; it relates to students whose faith *did* stick. Researchers found that students who have ongoing, caring, authentic relationships with five or more Christian adults outside their peer group are **considerably** less prone to walk away from their faith. Students relying almost exclusively on their peers for spiritual encouragement were most vulnerable.

Benefiting from their extensive research, we like to turn the 'five' spotlight on the Encore Generation. **Who are the FIVE (or more) young people in whom we invest time, prayer, care, and attention?**

They don't have to be high school kids getting ready to graduate. They may be younger than or beyond high school, but there is an army of younger people out there who need to know we are interested and care about them. Some are in our extended families, but many, especially those from non-Christian homes, need Christian adult relationships from outside their families.

Of course, we must protect kids from adult predators who might use a pretense of faith as an inroad to something perverse and deplorable. And even if our hearts are pure and innocent, we must guard ourselves from compromising situations. The inability to trust some adults with young people is a huge impediment to ministry between generations, but it shouldn't stop us in our tracks.

We must be willing to work under the children and youth ministry guidelines, authorizing background checks, getting fingerprinted, interviewed, or whatever a ministry might require for their protection and the protection of minors.

Some screening may seem as nonsensical as an airport security search of elderly passengers physically struggling even to make it on a plane. At some point, common sense should prevail, and hopefully you won't face undue scrutiny. But be a willing and ready participant.

HALF TWO — DAY TEN

It's really nice to know that careful research underscores how these principles of Scripture really do work. And there are so many leaders working with those younger who have a deep appreciation for the role the Encore generation can play in helping younger kids, adolescents, and emerging adults become true disciples, with faith that doesn't waver.

These aren't adults who only help fund upcoming youth trips. These Christians can make lasting impact through intentional, dynamic relationships.

And then, beyond the screening, some intergenerational ministries will have other guidelines. Group activities in public settings have more lenience. One-on-one ministry will typically demand more safeguards including parental permission, especially if minors are involved.

Like pre-trip inoculations that you'll bravely endure to see a new country's beauty, keep the connecting-with-younger-people reward at the forefront of your mind. They are worth this extra effort.

Giving It the Old College Try

As *somewhat* older people, Judy and I have enjoyed becoming friends with visiting international scholars and their families at the University of California at Santa Cruz, partnerships facilitated through the ministry of *International Students, Inc.* The ministry encourages us to interact face-to-face with our students at least monthly, allowing strong friendships to develop.

Instead of building an itinerary of special activities, we learned simply to invite these students and their families into the ebb and flow of our everyday lives.

Because our travel schedule sometimes takes us out of the area for long stretches, we have not had perfect marks every month. One Saturday we returned home to a kind email from our Chinese friends (raised as Communists and atheists), asking if they could meet us the next day at our home church. How special that they invited us to our own home church, where they have attended several times. Together we've had many good conversations about Christ, and their friendship has blessed us.

Many other adults in our church and community have become friendship partners with visiting international students and scholars. As these *Young Enough to Serve* adults share about their lives, it's fun to notice their voice inflection and excitement when talking about these international friendships. Obviously, they make a spiritual difference in the lives of these younger students, and the students add so much texture, depth, and purpose to older adults' lives.

Our home church, Christian Life Center, is a smaller midsize church with between one and two hundred currently attending. Imagine the exciting dynamic when a few dozen students from the Asian American Christian Fellowship[60] (also at UCSC) recently began attending our church.

We asked their student leader, Nick, what drew them to our church, and he said that the presence of many older adults was a huge draw. "We're around our peers all week long. It's nice to come into a congregation where multiple generations are present, active in worship, and open to engaging with us."

Ryan Moore, our pastor (in his thirties), asked Nick what our church could do for these students, expecting he might say something like add a fog machine during worship or provide a van to help with transportation. Instead, he answered, **"If you could help us establish relationships with older adults in your church, that would be at the top of our list."**

This was one of those *"Hallelujah-Aha!"* moments when we saw the hand of God giving us a huge gift, and we're having a blast taking an active role in making sure these connections happen.

God bless the Asian community for seeing the Church as an intergenerational family and for recognizing their need during college years to still stay connected to every generation. The need exists in every culture, but because of their cultural heritage, they appear to recognize the void more quickly and value older adults more deeply.

As invigorating as college communities are, they can become peer bubbles. One of the best gifts we can give college students and ourselves is a chance to step outside our respective peer bubbles and experience life in broader dimensions.

And we don't have to rely on the 'cool' factor. As pointed out in *Growing Young*, warm and genuine relationships are the new cool.

Growing Older

The above discussion focuses more on older churches growing young as a church—by keeping young people in the crosshairs of their scope.

Strange as it might sound in our youth-oriented culture, many churches full of young people could use some help 'growing older'.

Some churches that have focused so deliberately on reaching younger generations, including young families, may have intentionally or inadvertently de-emphasized the value of older adults in the process. In some churches with long histories, the pendulum may have already swung so far that the more seasoned adults have already found the exit door in droves. Some felt forced out with the loud music, and others sensed they could simply no longer identify with the new direction of the church. This, of course, goes against the grain of valuing every generation in the process of growing young.

Churches that have done a masterful job in clearing their pews of older adults may still have a Boomer remnant who have chosen to weather the storm and hang in with the younger congregation. But for the most part, these churches lack the gray and white hair fountains of wisdom that could add significantly to their understanding of life and faith, particularly the road ahead.

Like 'hipsters' overtaking some of our cities in America, *gentrification* is also common within churches, a slow and methodical shift that sends prior residents looking for a new home elsewhere.

Besides waiting for the current congregation to get older, what steps might younger churches take to add new life and vitality at the other end of the age spectrum?

Consider the saga of Virginia's McLean Bible Church[61] — commonly known as '*MBC*'. It faced such a challenge in one of its significant church ministries that catered to *Twenty Somethings* at their Tyson Corner campus.

Many of these young people were part of *Frontline*, a church within the larger church, with its own separate staff and a Sunday night service specifically targeting young adults. However, as a downside of *Frontline's* narrow age span, many young believers and seekers came up empty-handed when they asked to be linked to older mentors.

While reaching out to an amazing number of young adults—four thousand at its peak—some of these MBC young adults were deferring until their thirties a broader church life experience, transitioning from age-segregated ministries as children to youth to college to *Frontline*.

Because *Frontline* became too self-contained and because meaningful, beyond-peer relationships were scarce, it disbanded a few years ago. These young adults were encouraged to attend a main MBC service at one of their five campuses in the Washington D.C. metro area.

Justin Orr, executive pastor of discipleship and shepherding, acknowledges that McLean became leaner, losing some of the *Frontline* crowd in this transition. But those who stayed really blessed the larger church. While his tenure at MBC started after this transition, Justin feels the church leaders made a good but difficult decision, enduring short-term pain for longer-term kingdom gains.

"We see ourselves as a collective covenant community," Justin emphasizes, "and the redistribution of *Frontliners* into the larger community has been healthy for them and for our church as a whole."

For a season, this disbanded cohort commonly sat together in large groups, but over time they melded more easily into the whole and also began attending small groups with broader age mixes. "These young adults are more committed to community than personality," Justin adds. "Their engagement has proven to be more stable than that of other age groups, less apt to fluctuate when high-profile speakers come and go."

Once young adult connections to the whole church were better established, MBC introduced *Citywide* as a young-adult

Sunday evening complement to their Saturday night or Sunday morning experience. This venue has a variety of formats, and it's clearly meant to augment the young adults' broader church engagement, not replace it.

But most predominately young churches don't have a mega-merge option at their fingertips. What can other young-without-old churches do to move forward in adding age breadth?

Let's start with our attitudes and presuppositions. Let's refrain from simplistic, narrow typecasting:

> *Adults over 50 retire, go on trips, golf, sit on porches and knit, spoil their grandkids, lose energy & take naps, attend potlucks, sing hymns, reminisce, talk continuously about medications and medical procedures, say 'enough already' with technology, gripe about their church and politics and fixed incomes and Millennials, struggle to maintain their homes, slip and fall, move into assisted living, connect with hospice, and die.*

Some of us as leaders may also need expectation realignment, praying and hoping for better. As my childhood pastor Fulton Buntain frequently reminded us, "Things we appreciate tend to get better; things we depreciate tend to get worse." This wisdom, of course, applies to people, too. Let's agree to stop treating older adults as:

- Energy zappers to be avoided like the plague,
- Needy individuals requiring specialized care entirely separate from the rest of the body,
- Retired and resented vagabonds who come and go as they please, seemingly impossible to lasso and corral,

- Nuisances who whine and nag about things inconsequential,
- Simple, kind, obsolete folks who deserve pity in the present and a condescending pat on the back for their past service and faithfulness.

Instead, let's project vision for the skills and potential many of these older adults already possess and for helping even more find their Half Two purposes, as well. They can become prayer warriors, servants, and disciple-makers who realize they need vital connections with younger generations.

If young churches truly want older adults to experience community with them, they need proactive strategies to attract and retain older adults. Without relying on transfer growth—welcoming sheep from other flocks—how can this happen?

1. **Never give up on reaching them.** Our culture, not the New Testament, suggests adults over thirty are largely unreachable. Be faithful in laying out the plan of salvation for both the young and old. And, for those older, we're certainly not talking about only deathbed conversions. Many have decades of life ahead to repeat the disciple-making cycle.

2. **Build on what you have.** If your church already has a handful of older adults, strategize with them—along with their grands and their friends—on what it will take to engage more of their peers.

3. **Go for the disenfranchised.** Many older, currently unchurched, Christian adults have responded to ageism's cold shoulder by staying home on Sundays — settling for a TV, radio, or podcast church service. Consider reaching out to them through advertising and other means. "If you don't have a home church, we have young people in our congregation who need your godly wisdom and stories of God's faithfulness."

4. **Broaden your hearts.** It may stroke your ego to surround yourself only with hip, energetic, young people. But don't stop with only the younger slice of the pie. Engage them to reach out to every age demographic with deep and sincere compassion. Use natural strengths of your young congregation to help older adults. Provide platforms for reverse mentoring — in technology, for instance.

5. **Broaden your family definition.** Go after families, not just 'young families'. Most families I know are blessed with grandparents, aunts, uncles, and sometimes great-grandparents and even great-greats.

6. **Go to where they are.** You'll meet some of them on golf courses, at seniors' community centers, in hospitals. Some live in assisted living, 50+ communities, and in homes in your neighborhoods — that young volunteers from your church could help spruce up. For those who no longer drive, consider helping with errands or arranging transportation to your church. Conduct services at rest homes, or have musicians/prayer teams

from your church go from room to room. If you're a credentialed minister, make yourself available for funeral services at local mortuaries. Many of those grieving loss are older.

7. **Consider the age breadth of your worship.** You wouldn't invite Grandma to your home for Thanksgiving and then blast her away with obnoxiously loud music. Be sensitive to the needs of the whole. Make sure your worship leaders know they are not leading a youth rock concert. Neither are they there to cater only to grandma. Find a joyful, inclusive, God-honoring medium—with an age-diverse worship team that engages the unchurched as well as the churched.

8. **Don't over-rely on technology.** Don't assume that everyone in your congregation can connect through the internet or their smartphones to track upcoming events. Consider other avenues for communicating with the technologically challenged—and avoid tiny fonts and busy backgrounds.

9. **Improve physical access.** Proactively address access for physically challenged adults and others, not only to "the service" but also to valuable opportunities for serving and intergenerational influence. Even if our government has not enforced full ADA (*Americans with Disabilities Act*) compliance for your older church buildings, take healthy steps in that direction. 'Grandfathered in' compliance may keep your compliant grandfather out.

10. **Preach to the whole.** Younger congregations need to hear how they might encourage and influence those older, while opening their hearts to learning from more seasoned sojourners. As your church's age horizons expand, remember to use life stories and illustrations that relate to broader age ranges.

11. **Go for the Young Old.** Baby Boomers and the leading edge of Generation X are in significant transition years, trying to make sense of the empty nest, grandparenting, retirement, care for elderly parents, volunteering, downsizing, Social Security, etc. Use these transition points to reach out to them.

12. **Engage those older.** Don't settle for patronizing *"glad you made it to church"* pats on the back. These adults can do much more than warm pews, tithe, and pass out bulletins. Look for ways to mobilize them, using their experience and wisdom. As we have reinforced throughout this book, help them connect to your younger generations. People know when they are being used and when they are truly valued. Excel at valuing them.

✓ Identify some young people in your extended family with whom you've fallen out of touch. Ask God to help you break through the silence.

✓ Name your kids, grandkids, nieces, and nephews living far from you. Do you hope and pray mature Christian adults in their geographic area will become engaged in their lives? How can you answer that same prayer others might be praying for their younger relatives living in your area?

✓ How will you reach out to kids in your church coming from non-Christian homes, those who need a better firsthand look at what sustained faith looks like down the road?

✓ If you're from a predominantly younger church, what outreach-to-older-adult strategies seem most applicable and sensible?

Day 11. MARKETPLACE

Pastor of Costco

I promise you what I promised Moses:
'Wherever you set foot, you will be on land I have given you —'
Joshua 1:3 (NLT)

SEVERAL DECADES AGO, A DRINKING WATER SALESMAN dropped by our church office and spoke with one of our pastors. Responding to a question about the parameters of his sales territory, he said, "Really, wherever I plant my feet, that's my beat."

The significance of his response quickly registered with our pastor, and the next Sunday he admonished us as Christians to consider that wherever we plant our feet, that's our beat, too. Our hearts need to be open to opportunity wherever we go.

Those of us in professional ministry positions must remember that the radius of our beat extends much farther than the scope of our carefully crafted mission and vision statements and certainly beyond the walls and halls of our churches.

Jesus' parable of the Good Samaritan poignantly reminds us of professional ministers (a priest and Levite) who avoid helping a robbed, beaten, and left-for-dead man along the road. Their feet walked right by the man on the way to their formally assigned ministry beat.

Adopt a Building

Several years ago, we were introduced to the Adopt-a-Building ministry of City Impact[62] in San Francisco. Founder Roger Huang details the story of City Impact's rich history in a powerfully inspiring book, *Chasing God*[63].

> One early morning in 1984 after getting off the graveyard shift, Roger Huang was waiting for a tow truck in the Tenderloin. He noticed a young boy being picked on by a group of bullies. Torn between intervening to help the boy and not wanting to get involved, he drove away with a heavy heart.
>
> On the way home God laid the burden on his heart, "What if that was your son being picked on?" The next morning Roger and his wife Maite made 50 sandwiches, and Roger went back to the Tenderloin to give them away to the homeless that same day. The following week he brought Maite to the Tenderloin to help with the ministry, and San Francisco City Impact was born.
>
> Today, the ministry has grown to five major departments with 16 weekly programs. Everything they do is to intervene on behalf of the people in the inner city of San Francisco.

Francis Chan and his family were among the initial collaborators in the Adopt-a-Building ministry in San Francisco's Tenderloin district. Instead of expecting the Tenderloin residents of the 500+ housing projects to find their way to a church building, City Impact has adopted twenty-one local buildings and established churches within these buildings.

On one occasion, we visited building residents with the Chan's daughter Mercy, thirteen years old at the time. How rich for our intergenerational team, from 13 to 60+, to be led around the Tenderloin by this amazing young teenager! We saw firsthand the bonds of friendship between Mercy and these older residents. She not only knew their names—they knew each other on a personal level.

As we knocked and patiently waited at one door, Mercy told us that this resident was blind and would take a bit longer. When he unlatched the deadbolt, they warmly greeted each other by name. After some brief catching up, Mercy promised to return soon with a cup of coffee, reciting from memory exactly how he liked it prepared.

Through Mercy and others like her, these residents have experienced the merciful love of Jesus in words, friendship, and action. And once again, we too experienced the life-enriching joy of serving alongside younger generations—and learning from them.

For the most part, the building owners don't ask City Impact to intervene with their residents. The process starts slowly as the church reaches out and builds trust over time, knocking on doors, providing food, responding to other needs, and praying. Eventually these sites become formally adopted, and a minister is assigned and mentored, sometimes even someone from within the building.

We love this model of evangelism; instead of simply

inviting people to come to church, the church goes to where the people live and initiates relationships. Their broad vision has inspired ministry partners from many churches and denominations around the Bay area, and some churches have replicated their Adopt a Building ministry in other areas of the country.

Target Your Market

Inspired by their proactive example, Judy applies this adoption principle to her daily life. Instead of entering Starbucks, Costco, or Safeway simply as a customer, she purposes in her heart to enter those places as the self-appointed Pastor of _____. Certainly, Costco hasn't formally recognized her as Pastor of Costco. They aren't paying her; she ends up paying them for the opportunity. She is an unsanctioned, undercover pastor, and she knows in her heart that's her role for those thirty to sixty minutes of shopping.

She's not looking only for good deals. She looks for customers and staff who might need a smile, word of encouragement, or even a bit of humor. One day she stood behind a man who had a dozen basketballs in his cart. She started the conversation with, "Okay, I've narrowed it down to two options. You're either a basketball coach, or you lost your backboard." She has fun coming up with creative ways to break the ice.

She is intentional about calling people by name and asking about their lives. While it's not usually practical or polite to pray for cashiers at the checkout counter, if they speak of a need, she promises to pray for them before driving out of the parking lot, and she'll check in with them next time she is in the store.

HALF TWO — DAY ELEVEN

It's inspiring to see people 'on mission' doing the normal stuff of life. After all, life is made up of a whole lot of normal. As tantalizing as missions trips and ministry events can be, we absolutely don't want to ignore opportunities right around us.

And 'normal' days are certainly more exciting when we purpose in our hearts to be alert and ready for new conversations and special moments of opportunity. Sure, sign me up, Walmart is about to get an undercover pastor!

One Safeway cashier shared that her husband had recently passed away. Judy quickly stepped behind the counter, gave her a hug of support, and promised to treat her to lunch, which she did in the week that followed.

If you're simply a consumer, you may easily toss your receipt after the cashier asks you to go online to evaluate his or her service. But if you're that cashier's pastor, of course you affirm as requested and even let him or her know that you did so next time you're in the store.

We love how others have adopted this mindset. It doesn't

require years of college and seminary … just an attitude of the heart.

Judy and her four Popineau brothers are all credentialed ministers, influenced by growing up in a home with parents who knew what it meant to let their lights shine wherever they went. These adult kids still cherish memories of time spent around the dinner table as their dad, a residential house painter, told stories of how he had shared Christ earlier that day—as he painted, estimated jobs, or visited the paint store.

Before Judy's family of seven showed up to a party, she and her brothers always heard from their parents, *"Remember, be friendly to everyone."* This was great training, remembering that everybody matters, and being intentional about reaching beyond their smaller circle of friends mattered, too.

Now I, on the other hand, have to fight the urge to do all of our banking and most of my shopping online. I may even wander over to the self-serve checkout line at some stores, and of course, in most states we pump our own gas. If we're not careful, we might even make it through a whole day without talking to anyone we don't know.

Seriously, most of us could stand to move our intentionality up several notches when it comes to personal contact. It's not only our kids and grandkids affected by an automated world that has become more and more impersonal and tethered to technology.

Further ramping up her intentionality as pastor of whatever store she is in, Judy now disciplines herself not to look at her cell phone in checkout lines. Fixing our eyes on our smart phones signals to others that we're not available for conversation.

Let's recognize the many mission field opportunities at our disposal. Let's remember that our identity as followers of Christ and fishers of men should far outweigh our objective to be efficient shoppers, consumers, or patrons.

We invite you to a new level of deliberateness as you step into the marketplace. You may not have official pastor credentials, but you have God-given authority to be a minister wherever you go. God will put people in your path who need an encouraging word from you.

Let's purpose in our hearts to become more alert to the opportunities around us.

✓ Where in the marketplace can you envision your light shining more brightly? What will you do to become more intentional?

✓ Are you addicted to your smart phone to the degree that you disregard personally connecting with people? Sometimes even with your own family? It may not take a full 12-step plan, but what practical boundaries can we set to loosen overly tight grips on our smart phones?

Day 12. ARCHITECTURE

Another Great Fixer Upper

Unless the LORD builds the house, those who build it labor in vain.
Psalm 127:1a (ESV)

BUILDING OVER A THOUSAND HOMES, my dad was a respected building contractor in my hometown of Tacoma, Washington.[64] It's a heart-warming tribute to still see *"Wick-built"* homes advertised as a sign of quality, as they are re-sold many decades later.

My parents helped each of their eight kids get into their first home. Because I left Washington for California in my mid-twenties, I didn't get to move into a new, Wick-built home. Besides apartment living, Judy and I have resided in two homes, both previously occupied.

My father-in-law's background as a residential house painter and talented handyman was invaluable as I adjusted to an unfamiliar, fixer upper paradigm. He graciously helped us upgrade both homes.

In our first-home hunt in Diamond Bar, California, I was

ready to quickly rule out the pea-green-and-brick hillside home simply because of the exterior color. Judy's dad helped me see hidden potential behind ugly paint and overgrown shrubs. He likes to offer both solicited and unsolicited advice, starting with a *"what-you-need-to-do"* preamble.

Evaluating the structural integrity of these older homes was important. Paint is relatively inexpensive, but you don't want to slap it on a poorly constructed home and just hope for the best.

Home makeover shows on HGTV can make projects look initially hopeless but then increasingly promising after 'demolition day'. The stars of the show confront disasters with incredible design and construction acumen.

Property purchases go through without contingencies or lengthy escrows; the house is vacant; the construction materials, tools and workers are all in place; bureaucratic snags get resolved quickly; new owners stay away until the project is finished; and they never seem to run out of money before bringing projects to successful completion.

Beautifully and effortlessly homes are staged. Even the weather seems to cooperate. And it all comes together on our screens in less than an hour. Miraculous.

A Lord-Built House

I love the song by Roger G. Lentz[65] with this title and the Psalm 127:1 passage that inspired it.

As proud as I may be of my dad's legacy and *Wick-built*

homes, there is nothing like a Lord-built house. Once my dad sold homes and gave keys to new owners, his work at those addresses ended. The foundations were solid, and walls were square, but it was now up to the owners to maintain their homes and nurture the family within.

It's so vital that we look to the Lord to build our lives, our families, and our church families.

We can't simply sign the contract, take the keys, and be on our own merry way. The Lord wants to continue building his best within us and within our families, including our church families. This entails leaning heavily on God's Word, prayer, the Holy Spirit, and the counsel of other Christ-followers.

Without His construction and remodeling, we labor in vain.

Jesus looked hard at them and said, 'No chance at all if you think you can pull it off yourself. Every chance in the world if you trust God to do it.' Matthew 19:26 (MSG).

Works in Progress

Some of you have started your church's Half Two ministry from scratch. You're not tearing into a century of cherished history and protected family heirlooms. At the same time, you may be approaching the task at hand with little or no established resources. This, too, can require some scrappy foundational work, sometimes even more challenging when you look over your shoulder and see over-the-top financial investment in ministry at the younger end of life.

It reminds me of when our boys learned that their grandpa dug his first home foundation by hand (i.e. without bulldozers). "Really?" one of them asked with a look of surprise. "He didn't use a shovel?"

More typically, you're working with an established ministry. You may be confronting elements of your programs that have grown a bit routine and stale.

You might also find it difficult to consider changes or disruption of ministry when you factor in the expectations and fragile health of many in your group. Some are on the verge of breathing their last breath, and the mobility of others is increasingly limited. Demolition day seems too extreme for this age group. You might bring in a new speaker or musician, but you're leery about touching your basic program formats.

Meanwhile, the 'Young Old' (loosely defined now as *fifty to seventy*, subject to change when my peers and I turn seventy) fail to respond to countless invitations to integrate with your 'Fifty-Plus' group, ignoring both personal and generic invites. You're tempted to abandon this younger side of the age continuum and focus only on the elderly who need and appreciate your care.

Just as your creative juices are drawn to more *Young Old* inclusion, someone's health takes a turn for the worse. A once-faithful assistant goes into hospice, and you need to plan a memorial service for another dear saint who outlived most of her doctors.

While writing this book's final chapters, I endured five

nasty colds in succession. Judy came down with pneumonia, which eventually led to an overnight stay in the hospital. That same week, three incredible patriarchs from our relatively small church died on three consecutive days.

As we grieved for others and as our own energy levels, creativity, and sociability briefly sputtered downward, the Lord gave us extra empathy for many of you with chronic health issues—who feel you're doing your best just to maintain. It really is tough to dream big dreams when you're not well.

Be Aware of the Bubble

I'm tempted to say, "Beware of the bubble," but it's not something always to avoid. Our nuclear family may share the same socio-economic standing, ethnicity, country of origin, doctrinal beliefs, and maybe even the same political party. We don't need to apologize for this or run from every bubble of homogeneity.

But, being aware, we don't want to insulate ourselves to the point we fail to connect meaningfully with the world outside our four walls. Sometimes our insulation is so thick we lose touch with how hot or cold it really is outside.

We need to engage in conversations outside our echo chamber. We are not the whole enchilada. Sometimes, it can be as simple as asking "how's your day so far?" of the older person ahead of you in the Starbucks line. It doesn't have to be a formal event. Real people also go to grocery stores, gas stations, and libraries. They walk their dogs regularly. A dog makes for an easy "hello" opportunity. We need to see such opportunity in everyday happenings. Again, it's the "church" going to the people wherever they are.

HALF TWO — DAY TWELVE

As we're about to head for home, I realize that it's time to roll up our sleeves. We may need to challenge the status quo, not through a hostile takeover, but through prayerfully listening and through not allowing ourselves to become complacent.

Have we helped create environments that unintentionally encourage complacency and generational separation? Can we introduce some new faces into the mix, helping all of us become disciples who make disciples?

Beware of Stones Thrown from Glass Houses

As ministry pioneers, we sometimes want to infuse a prophetic voice into our complacent culture, and shout, "Wake up!"

It's easy to throw rocks and just presume that it's part of our unique missionary message or a privilege stemming from our advancing years. We've also hurled a few stones we'd gladly take back and have found ourselves apologizing moments later for our insensitivity and stereotyping.

At one of our supporting churches, I razzed Christians who spend their retirement energies going on cruises. However, we're not retired and have been blessed to go on several cruises. At the end of our message, a dear couple approached me and shared that they go on two cruises a year, each time packing an extra suitcase filled with Bibles in multiple languages to share with the cruise staff. They have led many cruise workers to Christ. *Touché!*

Are you picking up what I'm putting down? *Cruises, golf, Words with Friends?* Truth is, I'm starting to pick up some of what I used to put down.

Our YES! promotional video (www.yestoserve.org/ted[66]) also pokes fun at the retirement leisure lifestyle, particularly golf and church-sponsored field trips to the Jelly Belly factory. Yet golf can be great exercise and an opportunity to deepen relationships. Many people have accepted Christ and mentoring in their faith, even on golf courses.

For the last nine years, men in our extended family have enjoyed annual four-day, uncle-nephew golf tournaments—very rich times of interaction, laughter, spiritual encouragement, and competition—now spanning five decades.

Family friend Jeff Bekendam has graciously hosted a couple of these golf tournaments.

Jeff shares, "It is so pleasing to see the bond between generations, watching uncles and nephews enjoying each other's company. It takes an investment of time away from busy schedules, but to see the love and commitment these men have for each other is priceless.

"I see spiritual mentoring taking place between uncles and nephews through morning devotions, through handling competition on the golf course, and through the laughter and joking at the dinner table. It's a joy for me to see this during their annual golf tournament."

And we know that church field trips often give people needed breaks from their routines and provide opportunities to socialize. They can encourage and help people through dark seasons—even introduce some to Christ for the first time.

It's our intentionality and willing surrender to Christ that often need stimulation, not so much questioning our specific destinations or modes of transportation. We can bring honor to Christ in lots of places. Leisure is not the enemy, but selfishness, self-absorption, laziness, apathy, and entitlement may be worthy of a rock or two.

Judy and I recently attended a Boomer Ministry Summit at The Villages[67] in Central Florida, the largest active 50+ retirement community in North America, with 157,000 residents and growing. Here again is plenty of fodder for speculating about what God thinks of this massive, generationally segregated, leisure-oriented community. But people moving here to 'enjoy the good life' are real people. Many need Christ and need to be encouraged and challenged. And godly influence can multiply rapidly in a close community like this.

It was a blessing to see our friends Chris and Kathleen

Holck plant a thriving church[68] in this unique setting. They are making believers in this *make-believe* paradise, just down the road from Disney World. Challenging adults to be fruitful for Christ, they continually remind them, "If you're not dead, you're not done."

With their motto of *"Play Hard. Pray Hard. Finish Well,"* members of this Florida church show their heartfelt passion to reach and unleash Boomers for Christ.

How Firm a Foundation?

Perhaps because we entered second half adult ministry in our early to mid-fifties, we felt disconnected from many of the ministry programs we encountered, programs supposedly built for adults fifty and over. It often felt like a subculture we wouldn't be excited about asking our peers to join.

Uncomfortable with the "senior" label, those of us in our fifties were kiddingly referred to as "seniors-in-training." And we weren't quite sure what we were being trained for. Shuffleboard?

Someone asked recently, "What makes you cringe?" Two quick examples sadly both involved worship.

One is being in a sanctuary with music blaring at such a high volume that it's physically deafening nearly everyone in the room, with older adults feeling the brunt of it more sharply.

Another cringe-inducing setting is being in a colorless room with fluorescent lights—mono-generational, mono-cultural, mono-denominational while singing hymns in monotone—and then having someone boldly proclaim this is a taste of what heaven will be like. Yikes! Please, Lord, say it ain't so!

Offering free earplugs in the first setting doesn't seem like a viable solution. An infusion of warmer lighting, more color, and peppier musical accompaniment in the second venue also doesn't go far enough. We need help on many levels to become more welcoming of generations outside our peer group.

We long to experience the joy of the international, intercultural, interdenominational, and intergenerational kingdom of God. That's the kind of heaven I look forward to. We're not going to be *neighbors* in heaven; we'll be one big, loving, and integrated family.

As leaders, we can't make people feel guilty for getting complacent and not making disciples. We need to change the eco-system around them so that disciple making becomes more necessary and natural, while offering practical tools and live examples of faith-sharing. Settling for quarantined environments—that separate new believers from those who have walked with Christ for a half century or longer—isn't the best formula for nurturing a strong, disciple-making community.

On many levels, the disciples before Acts 2 were a mono-cultural, mono-national, mono-generational group of guys. Even though they hung out with Jesus, they were a bit entrenched in their own Jewish customs and not always gracious to those outside their peer group. They pushed children aside who wanted to be near Jesus and asked who in their tight circle might be the greatest.

But from the day of Pentecost forward, it's exciting to see how the Holy Spirit helped them become more intercultural, international, and intergenerational. Denominations weren't around yet, but believers began showing more appreciation for diversity in the body of Christ.

If we don't get outside our cozy corners, we can become hoarders of the gospel. That's a sign we've set His design drawings aside. And Half Two is a terrible time to go dark, bury our gifts, or hoard.

✓ Have you become too comfortable with what's comfortable? Do you need to be 'ruined for the ordinary'?

✓ What would it take to stir you and those around you to new levels of compassion?

✓ Are you in a bubble? Whom could you invite to help pop your bubble and move your prayers into refreshing, new, less predictable territory?

Day 13. LATE ARRIVAL

Joe Capri's Story

Be joyful in hope, patient in affliction, faithful in prayer.
Romans 12:12 (NIV)

OUR LIVES WERE TOUCHED TO THE CORE in early 2014 when we met Erica Capri in Spokane, Washington, at the age of 80 ("and-a-half," she reminded us). It was only eight months after the passing of her beloved husband Joe.

Erica grew up as the daughter of a wealthy shipping magnate in Bremen, Germany. Her home was formal and respectable. Although rich in the things of this world, she felt lonely and empty in her heart, learning that material things were not enough to fill this void.

While enjoying a game of tennis as a young adult, she met an American diplomat named Joe Capri, who was serving at the American Consulate in Bremen in post-World-War-II Germany. Their friendship grew, and they soon married.

Joe's diplomatic position took them to new residences on

several continents. By outside appearances, their lives were interesting and glamorous. For the most part, Erica was content to live in her husband's shadow as the wife of a respected diplomat. But over time the glamor faded. An endless succession of cocktail parties helped lead Joe to alcohol addiction.

Their relationship deteriorated as alcoholism took its toll. It became so bad that Erica could no longer stand to live with Joe. They separated. Erica returned to Germany with the youngest of their three children while Joe was transferred to Sydney, Australia.

Erica's Redemption

Feeling lost as a mother of three with a failed marriage, Erica became increasingly despondent and seriously contemplated suicide. At one of her lowest points she grabbed a Gideon Bible from her shelf, one that her daughter had taken from a hotel room in Bangkok, Thailand, a couple of years earlier. Erica had never opened the Bible before. It opened to the 23rd Psalm: *The Lord is my Shepherd, I shall not want. He makes me lie down in green pastures. He leads me beside quiet waters. He restores my soul.*[69]

Erica had heard these words at funerals but hadn't realized they came from the Bible. She knew right then, though, that she needed a Shepherd, greener pastures, quiet waters, and restoration of her soul.

The Lord gave Erica an insatiable appetite for His Word, and she surrendered her life to God after immersing herself in that miraculous Book. She did not know any Christians in Bremen. The Holy Spirit was her only teacher in those first six months. The Word and Spirit helped her discover God's unconditional love.

Another Radical Transformation

Naturally Erica began praying in earnest for her estranged husband. She also asked the Lord to change her own heart, too. One day, she prayed fervently for a break in Joe's bondage to alcohol. In the middle of those prayers, the Lord blessed her with a reassuring sense of calmness.

At that precise time on the other side of the globe, Joe had his Scotch whiskey on his hotel dresser, getting ready to booze it up over the weekend. Miraculously, as he gripped the bottle, Joe had an encounter with the Lord, who told him to put the bottle down. Joe developed a sudden distaste for alcohol, and he poured the whiskey down the drain of his hotel sink.

Delivered instantaneously from his alcohol addiction, Joe was drawn into the loving embrace of Jesus. As he and Erica communicated long distance, Erica knew this was not just a ploy to win her back. It was the real deal. Our loving Savior had redeemed his life, like Erica's.

Pilgrim to Settler

Joe and Erica's marriage was restored, and they re-united in Taiwan as Joe completed what turned out to be his final assignment as a foreign diplomat. He retired at fifty-nine.

Because their daughter was attending Eastern Washington University, they purchased a home in the Spokane area, where Joe and Erica lived for the next 30-plus years and where Erica continues to reside.

As new believers, they committed themselves to faithful study in the Word, prayer, and church attendance. As a Christian delivered from alcohol abuse, Joe was infinitely more pleasant to live with. The Lord healed the pain of their past. Through God's gift of forgiveness, his and Erica's hearts were knitted together as one.

At the same time, though, Joe began to immerse himself in watching sports on television, particularly American football, one of the luxuries alluding him in his many years living overseas. He spent considerable time over the next decade, from age 60 to 70, sitting in his recliner, remote in hand, with his eyes glued to the TV.

Erica admitted that she found Joe's newly adopted retirement lifestyle quite annoying. It was disappointing to see so many hours wasted as he settled into his personal comfort zone, far removed from action that really mattered. But Joe continued to grow in his knowledge of the Word and was eager to go to church whenever the doors were open. For that Erica was grateful.

Correction and Re-Direction

When Joe was seventy, he and Erica had an evangelist, Deanne, staying in their home. One evening they hosted a Bible study with over twenty friends in attendance.

In the middle of the study, Deanne sensed God was asking her to publicly share a particular word with Joe. Deanne disclosed that the word she received from the Lord was harsh and that she felt reluctant to share it.

As a younger adult, a female, and as a guest in the Capri home, she had plenty of reasons for being hesitant. And Joe was a feisty Italian, complete with all the machismo you might expect. But Deanne plowed ahead and wisely asked Joe for permission to share the word the Lord had placed on her heart. Thankfully Joe gave Deanne the green light.

She then boldly shared this revelation: "Joe, the Lord has impressed on my heart that you have made an idol of television and football. And if you're unwilling to get out of your recliner and serve Him, He will take you home."

Beyond the nerve it took for Deanne to share this bold word of warning, it took even more courage for Joe to receive this ultimatum with a teachable spirit. Joe was a very direct individual, and God knew that he could handle this stern admonition.

On the Monday morning following this weekend encounter, Joe placed a call to a friend who served at the Spokane County jail. He asked if he could become a volunteer through the chaplain's office. He was assured that there was both a need and an open door. He went through preliminary training and began serving even as he pursued his ministerial credentials, and he eventually became the assistant chaplain at the jail, going there faithfully five days a week.

Joe's life and daily agenda had been turned right side up, and the inmates loved Joe's sincerity, discernment, and direct approach.

One after another, God used Joe to help turn men's hearts to Christ. He also shared with female inmates. Early on he prayed he would live long enough for a thousand souls to turn to Jesus. He kept a running log of names. When he reached a thousand, he asked the Lord for another thousand.

Because of his international diplomatic work, Joe was fluent in four languages, which proved to be a huge asset in the jails. And because he knew firsthand Christ's power to deliver from addiction, he could find common ground quickly.

He could also sense when he was being played. Joe gave Bibles to the men who invited Christ into their hearts. Later he helped many of them secure glasses to help with their reading. When some men wanted to just exploit the vision care, he would call them on it. "You're not yet earnest about your faith. You just want free glasses. Get serious about Jesus and your walk with Him, and then come and see me for glasses."

Many times, he entered the jail lobby shouting loudly with a smile, "Somebody give me a box! I feel a sermon coming on!" He would then share a message from his heart.

Some of the more hardened and dangerous criminals were

on the sixth floor. Most volunteers were afraid to enter these cells. But Joe pushed his fears aside, never looked at anyone's rap sheet, and entered these cells alone with the steel-barred door locking behind him. Many of these intimidating men also surrendered their lives to Jesus, and their lives were transformed.

One by one and sometimes in groups, more and more inmates gave their hearts to Christ. At eighty-eight, Joe suffered a stroke and was confined to a wheelchair. With the assistance of friends, however, he visited the jail for another two years, always looking for opportunities to lead others to Christ.

Final Tally

After Joe's death, the chaplains and Erica reviewed Joe's monthly logs, which listed by name and date the men (and women) he had led to Christ. Some months, he had documented more than eighty names; other months, tallies were in the thirties.

In the final account of Joe's twenty years of jail ministry from ages seventy to ninety, Joe had led **just over ten thousand** inmates to Christ.

While some seed no doubt fell on hardened soil that never fully took root, Joe's faithful proclamation of the Good News of Jesus greatly influenced thousands of lives. And many of these converts have gone on to lead countless others to Christ.

As Erica pushed through the pain of grief in losing her best friend, she knew there were still many more lives to touch with the redeeming power of Jesus. This redemption can bring eternal life, break through addiction, mend broken hearts, restore marriages, light a fire under complacent Christians, and touch the most incorrigible of criminals.

As Erica remembers anniversaries of Joe's passing, she herself is challenged to stir up her gifts within as she asks the Lord, "What's next?" In her ninth decade of life, Erica still wants to make a difference.[70]

HALF TWO — DAY THIRTEEN

Are you kidding me? Is this kind of transformation and multiplication really possible in these later years of life?!

Meeting Erica and hearing Joe's story has got to be one of the highlights of our vision trek.

And the Legacy Continues

A few months after his father's passing, Joe and Erica's son Alex was visiting his mother in Spokane from out of state. Following his visit, he took a taxi to the airport. The taxi driver was a tough-looking guy with an interesting display of tattoos on the back of his head and neck.

Before even getting out of his mom's driveway, Alex asked, "Excuse me, sir. I can't help but notice that you've got a lot of ink going on there. May I ask you a question?" With the driver's permission, Alex continued, "I know this is a tacky question, but did you ever serve time?"

"Yep, sure did," the driver replied.

"Did you do any time at the Spokane County jail?" Alex inquired.

"Yes. Guilty as charged. Why do you ask?"

Getting to the heart of the matter, Alex probed further, "Did you ever meet a man named Joe Capri?"

At the mention of Joe's name, the driver stopped the car, sat bolt-upright, turned his shoulder, and inquisitively exclaimed, "You're Joe Capri's son?!"

"Joe is the one who led me to a personal relationship with Jesus Christ. Since then I've been clean and sober for ten years. Over these years my whole family has now come to Christ. If it weren't for Jesus and Joe, I wouldn't be here driving this taxi. I'd likely be dead."

Such an incredible moment for Alex, seeing the legacy of his deceased dad now live on through this man and his family … making disciples who make disciples.

Reflections

As mentioned earlier, we met Erica in Washington State in January 2014. The timing was ironic, hearing about Joe making an idol of American football and television at the very same time the Seattle Seahawks were about to experience their first Super Bowl win.

The whole state was glued to their TVs, fixated on their explosive team. We Seahawk fans were *all in* with our '*12th Man*' flags, jerseys, and banners, watching our team soundly defeat Denver, 43-8.

As we visited Erica's home, I asked her if they had tossed out their television after the idolatry revelation. "No, it's still here," she said as she pointed to a small TV in the corner of the den. "He'd watch games occasionally, but TV lost its overpowering grip on him. He had much more important fish to fry from that point forward. Still, God used his interest in sports as a good connecting point with the inmates."

Judy and I have shared this story numerous times, not only because it's dramatic but also because it contains so many important reminders of God's readiness to move in the lives of the Encore Generation:

- Many adults in Half Two, with trappings of worldly success, wrestle with major brokenness.
- God delights in miraculously saving people over the age of fifty, with or without our best efforts.
- How quickly the pilgrims became settlers! This observation from a high school US history textbook[71] certainly applies here to Joe's more complacent seventh decade, in his sixties. It's a big challenge to keep us older pilgrims on the pilgrim track, or to get us back to our pilgrimage. But with God's help, it can happen.
- Even good, seemingly harmless things can keep us from God's best. In Matthew 6:19 (NLT) Jesus admonishes us, "Don't store up treasures here on earth, where moths eat them and rust destroys them, and where thieves break in and steal." As Joe lay back in his easy chair, the moths nibbled; his mind rusted; and time-robbers snatched his hours.
- God can use younger people to speak boldly into the

lives of older adults, with words of both encouragement *and correction*.

- God can use women to speak into the lives of men, and vice versa.
- God saves us, in part, so that we can reach others. His plan doesn't end with our becoming disciples. Disciples are meant to make disciples who make disciples!
- Joe's first redemption linked to his obediently pouring whiskey down a hotel sink. Joe's second redemption reveled in pouring himself into the lives of lost men and women.
- We need to raise the bar of expectation for Christians beyond 50, 60, 70, 80, and even 90. God's most productive days for us could quite possibly still be ahead.

In the last days, God says, I will pour out my Spirit on all people. Your sons and daughters will prophesy, your young men will see visions, your old men will dream dreams. Acts 2:17 (NIV)

- ✓ After hearing Joe's and Erica's testimony, are you inspired to take a break from your TV or from whatever else might be holding you back from wholeheartedly serving God? What holds you back or causes you to move more sluggishly than you need to?

- ✓ Or is God perhaps tapping you on the shoulder and asking you to deliver a challenge to someone stuck in idle? No matter what your age, step out in faith as a willing, bold, and tactful vessel of Christ but couple genuine encouragement with that correction.

Day 14. HEADING HOME

Finishing Well

In the same way, let your light shine before others,
that they may see your good deeds and glorify your Father in heaven.
Matthew 5:16 (NIV)

SIX OF MY SEVEN SIBLINGS AND I ATTENDED
and graduated from Seattle Pacific University[72], a Christian
university affiliated with the Free Methodist Church. Our
mom's brother, Dr. Roy Swanstrom, was chair of the history
department for a few decades. He was a highly respected,
legendary professor also known for being exceptionally
challenging and a tough grader.

Only one sibling, our sister Elaine, had the courage to take
one of his classes for credit. There was something extra
intimidating about the possibility of struggling in our uncle's
class. I chose to audit one of his European history courses to
experience his teaching—while sidestepping the fear of family
disgrace.

Looking back, I consider Uncle Roy as a favorite mentor.

Even though I didn't major in history, I enlisted him as my academic advisor. Our friendship grew even closer after college.

Do Something Conspicuous

At SPU, Uncle Roy founded the Centurions, a service and discipleship honorary comprised of junior and senior men. Started in 1959, this group flourishes still today, over fifty years later.

During my sophomore year, my uncle confided that he wanted to recommend me for membership in this select collegiate group, but I really hadn't done much yet to earn a spot. His advice to me was, "Do something conspicuous." It almost seemed conniving and out of character from my respected mentor and uncle, but it was necessary. I confess there was definitely some nepotism going on, but he knew I had dormant leadership qualities I needed to exercise and polish.

Aside from student government, decent grades, and participation on the rowing team, I can't remember what conspicuous roles I took on to justify my Centurion invitation, but my junior and senior college years became very special years of accelerated growth and leadership. Centurion role models surrounded me, and I deeply respected them. Dr. Swanstrom believed in my potential well before others recognized it, and for that I am eternally grateful … even if he was a bit biased.

We need to be that person in the lives of both the young

and old, with fresh eyes to see unrealized potential. Not only young people fly under the radar far below their capacity. We need to challenge shy and reticent older adults to do something conspicuous, not for personal glory or for entrance into an elite group, but for the glory of God and for the benefit of His kingdom.

It's easy to affirm outgoing, visible leaders who are already making an impact, but take the time to also recognize and encourage quieter individuals. With that affirmation, consider challenging them to next steps that can help open new or broader horizons.

I recommend face-to-face conversations that happen spontaneously or planned appointments over coffee or a meal. Of course, you can also affirm by phone, through social media, text message, letter or email, but look for two-way conversations that lead to healthy steps forward.

The Voice of Experience

We owe much to personal experience when we pass on advice and wisdom. My Uncle Roy, too, could look back at turning points where he had done something simple that set himself conspicuously apart and altered his life course.

After graduating from high school, he attended a local vocational school over the summer to learn shorthand. With the advent of new technologies, this skill has become increasingly rare. Even back in the thirties, shorthand was not a common skillset.

God used this newly acquired skill for a very surprising

assignment. A United States senator from Washington State, Homer T. Bone, contacted the vocational school and asked for names of male students who knew shorthand. Subsequently, my uncle worked for the senator the rest of that summer in Tacoma, WA, and then he became Bone's private secretary in Washington, D.C. for the next ten years.

Those ten years in the Beltway, along with military service during World War II, gave this Swedish immigrant a huge advantage as he later raced through his undergraduate work and Ph.D. So quickly, in fact, that he soon returned to Seattle Pacific and found himself teaching some of his younger college classmates.

"Little is much when God is in it." We never know how God might use something small to move us into roles we haven't yet dreamed of.

What Will Set You Apart?

One of CS Lewis' many books is *Surprised by Joy*[73]. Nineteenth century poet, William Wordsworth, wrote a sonnet by that same name[74] which later inspired Lewis' book title. In both the sonnet and the book, "joy" is the divine.

God delights in surprising us with His joy. Yes, He is the same yesterday, today, and forever—but we don't serve a stodgy, predictable God. Just when we think we have Him and life figured out, He surprises us with something new and fresh. Remaining open to God's creative, unscheduled surprises adds true, spontaneous joy to our lives.

Do you have a passionate interest or special gift that may

be useful in God's kingdom? If it's still in raw form, how can you develop it? Perhaps take a few classes, find a personal mentor, research your interests, watch *YouTube* tutorials, or get in touch with local churches, ministries, or non-profits to ask how you might use your skills there.

The open posture of new college graduates serves them well. While some are nervous about landing that *first real job*, most are eager to put their years of classroom study to use. We older kingdom workers would do well to emulate that same heart of openness and excitement.

We may be tempted to let our dreams go or avoid taking risks because of our age, our distance from education, the unorthodoxy of our pursuit, morning aches and pains, and other reasons. Remember, however, we also bring a lifetime of experience to the table.

Step Outside the Box

For my uncle, it was learning shorthand.

For Joe Capri, it was a call to the county jail, asking if they could use a volunteer.

For Cambodia-bound Seth and Cindy, it was a willingness to check out *ELIC*, a wonderful organization that opens doors to teach English as a second language abroad.[75]

For former high school Spanish teacher Art, it was 'flunking retirement' at age seventy to begin teaching junior high for the first time.

For Larry and Marilyn, it was taking their choir directing and accompaniment skills to their retirement community and starting an inspiring, creative, and beloved choir known throughout their county.

For Dean and Shirley, it was saying yes to serving as camp grandparents at Royal Family Kids Camp for ten years.

For Pat, it was going on her first missions trip at the age of eighty.

For Jackie, it was serving as a class grandparent at a local Christian elementary school in her mid-eighties.

For Kitty, it was starting her faithful service with *Meals on Wheels* at 67 and making her final deliveries at 94.

For June, it was sewing dresses for *Dress a Girl Around the World*, starting at age 90. 446 dresses sent so far!

For Russ, it is continuing to volunteer annually at *Gleanings for the Hungry*, now at the ripe age of 99.

The Great Commission starts with a short, two-letter word. *Go.* It requires movement. It's both sad and funny how some active, older adults have the courage and stamina to travel the world as tourists, but their confidence and physical energy quickly dissipate when asked to serve locally, regionally, or abroad.

For some of the frail elderly, the 'get up and go' already got up and went. In life's final stages, the going diminishes, from *Go-Go* to *Slow-Go* and finally to *No-Go*. In the No-Go phase, our living radius settles in much closer to home—or our homes move to environments with better physical access and amenities.

For those whose mobility is severely limited, "go" might now mean picking up the phone, sending cards and hand-written notes, becoming an online mentor,[76] or pouring a cup of coffee for a visiting friend.

One of our friends, Babe Sanborn, now deceased, made it a practice to give away a china cup and saucer to those paying her a visit. Her outside-the-home activities were limited, so she invited visitors to pick out a cup from her collection as an outbound, tangible reminder of Christ's love.

Opening Your Heart and Home

Judy's mother Peggy loves to practice hospitality, and she still exercises that gift often and well, now in her mid-eighties. My mother, no longer living, was also blessed with this same gracious gift.

For decades in their second half of life, my parents opened their home and served Swedish pancake breakfasts nearly every Saturday morning. It was an open invitation. Friends and family simply called ahead to let my parents know they were coming. Even last minute calls were welcomed. I can still hear my dad saying with some excitement as he'd hang up the phone, "Time to whip up some more batter; five more are coming!"

This was an incredibly special family tradition—with lots of warm and meaningful conversations around the breakfast nook. And the Swedish pancake tradition continues through their extended family, with literally thousands of pancakes served each year in the homes of their kids, grandkids, great- and great-great grandkids, now spanning several states.

As the *go* radius narrows in later years, hospitality can become a final bastion of outreach. Unfortunately, though, like cursive writing, hospitality has for many become an

American culture lost art.

Of course, receiving guests requires some effort. When people struggle to maintain, it's difficult to even think about entertaining others in their home.

But let's not think only of lavish, home-cooked meals and nicely decorated tables as synonyms for hospitality. It's not a gift reserved for home economics majors, *Pinterest* enthusiasts, or younger adults with boundless energy.

Hospitality starts in our hearts, as we make room for Jesus and others to enter our lives and make themselves at home. If we wait until our lives or homes are perfect, we miss the point and miss out on lots of opportunities to share Christ's love.

We are blessed to live in an area of the country people enjoy visiting. We love hosting out-of-town guests and local friends as well. Sometimes we admit to not being intentional enough about exercising hospitality. But every time we do it, our lives become richer.

We encourage you, as God gives strength, to offer hospitality to both close friends/family and to others you'd like to know better—like the neighbors down the street who have not yet set foot in your home.

It doesn't have to be a gourmet extravaganza. Keep it simple and do it more often. During warmer months, consider even coffee or tea on your deck, patio, or porch.

Let's invite others into our imperfect lives, and watch God do something fresh and exciting.

Or as Peter puts it in 1 Peter 4:9 (NIV), *Offer hospitality to one another without grumbling."*

Our Swan Song

If there ever were a season of life's urgency, we who are clearly in Half Two or life's final quarter should be keenly aware that the clock is ticking. Soon and very soon we are going to see the King. Our time is short, and of course, could be shorter yet with Christ's rapture of the Church. Or death could unexpectedly claim our fragile lives at any moment. We may not have months, years, or decades.

We love seeing boldness kick in at new levels as seasoned Christians realize their remaining time is limited. It's time to throw caution to the wind. This may be our last opportunity to share Christ with our neighbor or to follow through on some earlier calling.

In the lives of people coming to Christ after fifty, we've seen an enormous sense of this urgency. Moving from darkness to light more recently, they don't have time to grow complacent. Let's pray their steadfast spirit will contagiously infect us all.

Some may experience the 'swan-song' phenomenon, based on folklore suggesting that swans sing a beautiful song just before death, following a lifetime of mostly silence. Fine arts scholars can point to the work of numerous composers who showed a last burst of creativity just prior to death. While this phenomenon's legitimacy is not without critics, it presents a fitting metaphor for encores occurring in life's final stages.

I hope this book isn't my final swan song, but I confess that future uncertainties provide strong motivation. I wrote this book's dedication first, which gave me determination to complete *Half Two* (the book, not my life) while my father-in-law is still alive.

Then, too, Papa Don could outlive me. Our own personal prospects of physical decline, disability, dementia, or death can add more fuel to our fires. Let's bring closure to unfinished, worthwhile projects while our minds and bodies are still sound. This book will be around for my grandchildren and great-grandchildren to read, long after Jesus takes me home. Very gratifying.

Connect

Over half a century ago, disengagement theories of aging suggested that this half-two season is when we begin disconnecting from society, starting with retirement. In practice, this theory still has a few takers, but most social scientists today recognize that career detachment and aging do not have to lead down the quiet trail of withdrawal.

Certainly, as Christians we want a growing attachment to Christ, but this doesn't mean that we begin holding others at arm's length.

Love the Lord your God with all your heart and with all your soul and with all your strength and with all your mind; and, love your neighbor as yourself. Luke 10:27 (NIV) As Jesus commands us in Luke and also in Matthew and Mark, he offers no qualifiers to suggest this full-orbed love applies only to life's earlier, energetic years.

Relationship with others can actually accelerate during a good portion of our later years, especially with more breathing room in schedules, growing extended families, and relocation into communities with higher concentrations of people.

The importance of continued socialization is obviously good for physical, mental and emotional health. To me, though, the word 'socialization' weakly defines larger life. We must encourage relationships that grow well beyond our peer or comfortable social cliques, connecting with others in a much broader context.

May we always be champions for engaging in more meaningful ways with those different from us, including those well outside our peer, ethnic, socio-economic, and Christian silos.

The Pharisees criticized Jesus for hanging out with publicans and sinners. Jesus saved his greatest criticism for the Pharisees and religious leaders who over-insulated themselves in ivory towers, falling prey to what Howard Hendricks referred to as "the hardening of the categories."[77]

The same trap remains today. The bait has been set. Let's not succumb to living the life of a Pharisee or curmudgeon.

Communicate Hope

No matter how sinful and challenging you perceive today's world to be, refrain from negative, wet blanket comments such as, "I would never want to raise children in today's culture." That's a discouraging pathway and unsuited for building younger generation rapport.

Learn from the last question asked of Jesus—in Acts 1:6 (NLT)—before He ascended into heaven: *So when the apostles were with Jesus, they kept asking him, 'Lord, has the time come for you to free Israel and restore our kingdom?'*

Jesus didn't respond with, "You've got to be kidding. Things are going to get a whole lot worse before they get better. You guys are in for an exceptionally dark, rough road ahead."

Instead, He skirted the immediate 'yes' response they were seeking and went straight to a personal hope message that superseded the restoration of Israel. In Acts 1:7-8a (NLT), *He replied, 'The Father alone has the authority to set those dates and times, and they are not for you to know. But you will receive power when the Holy Spirit comes upon you ...'*

Yes, we may see significant spiritual erosion and signs that Jesus' return is closer than ever, but let's be ready always to point to the hope we have through the power of the Holy Spirit. And because of that hope, what a great time to be alive!

Bathe It with Prayer

We've discussed it earlier, and I'll repeat it now in closing. This season of life needs prayerful reflection and continued open conversations with God about where to turn next. It's so easy for social norms and the routines of life to take over. We need to ask God to direct us now, just as we needed His direction earlier in life.

Prayer is indeed powerful. God can move in us and through us in more profound ways if we stay desperate to hear His voice, not leaning on our own understanding. In **all** our ways and for **all** our days, we need to acknowledge Him. He will direct our paths.

Serve

If you type in "seniors" and "serve" in online image searches, you'll mostly see a lot of seniors being served, along with a few suited up for a game of tennis. The idea that older adults would actively and intentionally serve others is unfortunately still a bit elusive in our thinking, search engines, and in some of our churches.

When Jesus grabbed a towel and washed the disciples' feet, they were uncomfortable with Jesus serving them. Although slow to grab a towel themselves, they felt Jesus should be on the receiving end. His gracious, humble serving seemed topsy-turvy. Similarly, others will argue that this is our season primarily to be served.

Following Jesus' example, let's keep touching lives and

modeling servant leadership, as He gives us strength. This doesn't mean we rob others of the joy of serving and giving. We also need to be gracious recipients, as God directs.

HALF TWO — DAY FOURTEEN

Life is an incredible adventure. We don't know what "surprises" God will use, but we know He wants to use us. The Encore Generation has a broad life context and sees how earlier, small, seemingly inconsequential things became major life turning points.

Leaving this two-week vision quest, I know changes back home will help us make a deeper impact for Christ. So much untapped potential! We can do better! May God direct our steps!

If you annually face cold, harsh winters, consider redefining for your church what snowbirds do. Instead of lounging poolside in Arizona, consider serving a month or two in a warmer climate at a place like Gleanings for the Hungry in Dinuba, California. Each winter we rub shoulders with 'Mission Builders'[78] coming from colder climates to serve at this Youth With A Mission (YWAM)[79] base. We prepare dried soup mix that goes out with the Good News of Jesus to needy nations around the world. Our favorite timeshare.

Let's assume that Christ still has a purpose for us and wants us to serve Him and others. Start with a yes, a willing heart. Then let's figure out how this can happen, factoring in our limitations. Let's hang on to that servant's heart—even as some outreaches fall out of reach.

One of our favorite YES! heroes is Ward Hastings, a willing volunteer with whom we've worked side-by-side for the last ten years. He can no longer tackle the physical projects he took on in his early seventies, but he remains tenacious and resilient despite numerous physical challenges, including Parkinson's. Through his seventies he supervised teams of landscape volunteers that served at our home church and at other churches and ministries. Now eighty, he still assumes a leading role in encouraging international friendship partnerships at UC Santa Cruz.

Half Two Be the Church

This is not a season to become careless about church attendance. Stay engaged with your local church, as God gives you stamina.

Consider the negative effects that may ripple through generations when able-bodied Christian grandparents and great-grandparents view church as entirely optional for this stage of life. Sure, they may choose to travel more now than they did earlier in life when tied down to jobs. But *away from home* doesn't need to equate to *away from church*. Consider blessing other churches with your presence when you're away.

Your kids, grandkids, and great-grandkids are watching. They will learn from and often mimic your behavior. Display a contagious love for the local church and the broader

Church, the family of God.

Actively contribute to the life of your congregation. Find an avenue of serving in and through your church. Be an encouragement to your pastor and other leaders. Help build bridges between generations in your church. Be a part of a small group. Support your church with your tithes and offerings. Be blessed, and be a blessing.

And let's not forget those who are housebound or in care facilities who can no longer physically gather at your church building. Be intentional about regularly connecting with them. Some may still be able to make it to church services and just need help with transportation.

Judy and I enjoy inviting one of many spiritually and mentally alert, housebound adults to give the opening prayer when we speak at churches and conferences. With advanced notice, we call their land line from an iPhone, put them on speaker, and use the stage microphone to amplify their inspiring words and prayer. We encourage you to do the same in your church gatherings. You can step it up a notch with *FaceTime* or *Skype* if you're tech-savvy at both ends, but we've been blessed by the simpler audio-only approach.

Make Disciples ... With Help

When other pieces of the puzzle are in place (i.e. connecting, praying, serving, diligent study of God's word), we know that making disciples can flow more naturally. Christ did not restrict His Great Commission to His followers from a couple millennia ago. Let's not settle for less. He wants us to make disciples. We want to make disciples.

Making disciples may not have surfaced in your earlier repertoires and may seem out of place as an encore performance for you. But it's not too late to make it an integral part of your life.

In John 14, Jesus told His followers that He would not leave them as orphans but that He would send His Holy Spirit to comfort and equip them: *The Advocate, the Holy Spirit, whom the Father will send in my name, will teach you all things and will remind you of everything I have said to you.* John 14:26 (NIV)

Let's warmly embrace this promised Third Person of the Trinity, and allow the Holy Spirit to overcome any sense of personal abandonment or inadequacy. We have opportunities now, and the Word, Spirit, and God's Church will equip and empower us, allowing our lifetimes of experience, devotion, wisdom, and discernment to spill generously into the lives of others.

YES!

It's time to find our **ALL-CAPS BOLD and exclamation marks!** Let's move beyond observation to calling, beyond explanation to passion. We can't settle for a lowercase faith and a boring, predictable conclusion.

We have an uppercase **GOD** who wants to equip us in life's final stretch and to help us say *YES!* to finishing well.

Let's remember, we're in the process of ***completing well—***

not competing or retreating—**completing!** Let's add a sense of healthy completion to our lives, families, churches, neighborhoods, communities, and national/global witness.

Let's finish well the work to which God calls us.

✓ Most writers hope readers will glean at least one useful or profound takeaway from reading their books. Perhaps you have discovered something helpful that you can apply to your own life and to the life of your church. What opportunities do you see to make Half Two better?

Make It Count!

Please join us in making Half Two count—be that godly example, and help us by challenging and inspiring those around you.

We can do something about church decline in America. Let's become part of the solution, not part of the problem. And we pray that church leaders will see you as an ally, partnering with you to reach the lost.

It's a deep honor to share this journey with you. Thank you for joining us as we celebrate great things already happening for American adults in Half Two and as we also tap into dormant or quarantined—and amazing—potential.

May your stories honor God and captivate the rest of us; may they influence and multiply; may we all do something conspicuous. It's time to shine as together we make Half Two whole, make it His, and make it count. Eternity with Christ is just around the bend.

Let's live out encores He will applaud.

ACKNOWLEDGEMENTS

SERVING IN THIS SECOND-HALF MINISTRY ARENA, I find it ironic that I have no memories of living grandparents. But my own parents became grandparents when I was very young, giving me a close-up view of multi-layered, intergenerational family dynamics. And they exemplified generous, thoughtful, fruitful Half Two living that extended much longer than their parents' generation.

Both my parents and in-laws celebrated their 67th wedding anniversaries, with hopefully more to come for Judy's parents. What incredibly solid foundations of marital stability, Christian devotion, and longevity!

My mom's parents were Salvation Army officers in both Sweden and the United States. My maternal grandfather, Carl Swanstrom, penned detailed, perfect-English diaries of his young adult life in the Pacific Coast Marching Band, prior to returning to Sweden where his diaries revert to Swedish. He resumed his flawless English diction and penmanship when he spent his later years back in the Pacific Northwest.

I'm so thankful for my immigrant grandparents' passion for ministry and my grandfather's legacy of writing that dates to the nineteenth century—giving me the privilege of knowing him, quirks and all, long after his passing.

This meaningful, first-decade YES! adventure has, of course, been a collaborative effort with my wife Judy, who instigates and lives out much of what I write about in *Half*

Two. Being married to this amazing, caring, spiritually passionate woman for over 36 years is far more than I deserve. And marrying into the Popineau family has been incredibly delicious icing on the wedding cake.

In writing this book, I am *hugely* indebted to Julia Young, a former university English professor, who painstakingly edited, re-edited, and enhanced my work as a first-time book author. In my seventh decade of life, it's humbling to discover such considerable room for growth, which Julia patiently and generously helped uncover through this process.

Kudos, too, to Dan Pitts for our cover graphics.

Thanks to a wonderful cadre of second-half adult ministry colleagues who are already changing the ministry landscape, accentuating both the blessing and calling of these extended Half Two years.

We have some amazing prayer and financial supporters who have brought great encouragement and practical resources to sustain and grow the ministry of *YES!* Some of you, such as Lanette Henderson,[80] have given with significant personal sacrifice. And many of you praying and giving are well under fifty. Thank you!

And thanks to all who have invested time and energies serving on our board of directors, advisory board, and ministry teams throughout this past decade. As both young and older ministry pioneers, we have learned a lot together.

With heartfelt gratitude to those who have paved the way, we welcome those of you about to join us. Much more *Half Two* potential lies ahead!

ABOUT THE AUTHOR

BORN IN TACOMA, WASHINGTON, IN 1954, Wes Wick was the seventh child of eight, with he and his siblings evenly split between the Builder and Boomer generations. With the passing of his parents and his two brothers, Wes recently became the oldest surviving Wick male in this large, extended family—a bit sudden and unnerving for someone growing up next to the youngest.

A graduate of Seattle Pacific University, Wes double-majored in Business Administration & Economics and German language. He earned his M.A. degree in Social Science, with an emphasis in College Student Development at Azusa Pacific University. Later, in pursuit of ministerial credentials, he completed additional coursework at Vanguard University.

For a short stint in the late 70s, Judy Popineau served as Children's Pastor at Wes' home church, Life Center, in Tacoma—just long enough for the two of them to meet. Wes chased her down to Southern California, where they fell in love and then married in 1981. The next year Judy gave birth to twins, Jonathan and Heather. Three and eight years later, Andrew and Jeremy rounded out the *Sixwix* squad.

Over the last decade, eight new incredible family members have been added: three daughters-in-law, a son-in-law, and four grandchildren ... so far.

While serving actively in local churches, Wes has made his

career primarily in Christian college administration in California. He served at Azusa Pacific University as director of both *Communiversity* and New Student Orientation. At Vanguard University, he served as Admissions director for five years. He served another nine years at Bethany University in the role of registrar, followed by vice president for Advancement.

Between his years at Vanguard and Bethany, Wes served as a vocational rehabilitation consultant for over a decade, primarily helping workers with injuries return to work.

Wes and Judy's founding of *YES! Young Enough to Serve* in 2008 is well chronicled within this book. Subsequent to starting this interdenominational ministry, Wes and Judy became appointed US missionaries with the Assemblies of God.

Wes' love for writing didn't fully emerge until his fifties, and *Half Two* is his first book. With this book now complete, he plans to resume blogging more regularly.

An eight-year-old at heart, Wes is still in the growing-up process.

YES! RESOURCES

YES! Young Enough to Serve is committed to helping adults over fifty thrive both personally and collectively. YES! helps individuals and churches catch a deeper and broader vision for kingdom purpose in life's second half.

YES! emphasizes four mainstays worthy of full attention: **Connecting**, **Praying**, **Serving**, and **Making Disciples**—both inside and *outside* our peer group.

YES! is available to help churches in many ways:

- Speaking at conferences, retreats, churches, and other venues.
- Serving at multi-church events.
- Developing resources such as this book, podcasts, blogs, newsletters, website and other online tools that present practical, biblical, moving-forward solutions for life's second half.
- Partnering with young people to help encourage and challenge adults over fifty.
- Consulting with leaders online and through phone/video conferencing.
- Supporting national, regional, and local leaders in efforts to strengthen paradigms of second-half-adult ministry.
- Serving at the local church level to practically apply and model Scriptural principles championed through YES!

- Strengthening our base of prayer and financial support to reach more adults over fifty.
- Opening doors of opportunity for *Half Two* adults to become salt and light in their communities.
- Collecting and sharing stories of *Half Two* adults who are making a God-honoring difference in the lives of others.

PLEASE CONTACT US.
We'd love to hear from you.
www.**yestoserve**.org/contact
email: info@yestoserve.org
831-359-5308
Share *Half Two* with others: www.half2.org

NOTES

[1] After sharing the story of the Good Samaritan, Jesus said "Go and do likewise." Samaritan's Purse's mission is to follow the example of Christ by helping those in need and proclaiming the hope of the Gospel. Led by Franklin Graham. samaritanspurse.org

[2] Operation Christmas Child, samaritanspurse.org/what-we-do/operation-christmas-child/

[3] *Throwing Grandma and Grandpa under the Bus*, Wes Wick, 2009, yestoserve.org/yes-blogs/under-the-church-bus

[4] Amy Hanson, Ph.D. amyhanson.org. *Author of Baby Boomers and Beyond: Tapping the Ministry Talents and Passions of Adults Over 50*, published by Jossey-Bass, 2010.

[5] Ted Cunningham is the founding pastor of Woodland Hills Family Church in Branson, Missouri.

[6] Ally Bank *Tech Grandkids* Commercial, youtube.com/watch?v=3UnYPtSnOJY

[7] International Student Inc.'s website address is isionline.org.

[8] Grandma Moses, en.wikipedia.org/wiki/Grandma_Moses

[9] Halftime: Moving from Success to Significance by Bob Buford. Published by Zondervan. amazon.com/Halftime-Significance-Bob-P-Buford/dp/0310344441. Also see halftimeinstitute.org

[10] Demography of the United States, en.wikipedia.org/wiki/Demography_of_the_United_States

[11] Stanford Center on Longevity, longevity.stanford.edu

[12] Full quote from Wikipedia: *"Our new Constitution is now established, and has an appearance that promises permanency; but in this world nothing can be said to be certain, except* **death and taxes**.*"*— Benjamin Franklin, in a letter to Jean-Baptiste Leroy, 1789

[13] *Third Calling: What are you doing the rest of your life?*, by Richard and Leona Bergstrom, published by Re-Ignite, a division of ChurchHealth, 2016. re-ignite.net

[14] Dr. Henry Cloud Quotes: goodreads.com/author/quotes/1114699.Henry_Cloud

[15] *The Intergenerational Church: Understanding Congregations from WWII to www.com*, Peter Menconi, 2010.

[16] MOPS Mothers of Preschoolers, mops.org

[17] *Sticky Faith: Everyday Ideas to Build Lasting Faith in Your Kids*, Dr. Kara E. Powell & Dr. Chap Clark, published by Zondervan, 2011. fulleryouthinstitute.org/stickyfaith

[18] *Growing Young*, Kara Powell, Jake Mulder, and Brad Griffin, Fuller Youth Institute, published by Baker Publishing Group, 2016. churchesgrowingyoung.com.

[19] I've attributed this quote to Peter Drucker because I heard him say it in a lecture back in the seventies, but I haven't found that quote appearing in print. Nonetheless, I like it. Peter Drucker was an Austrian-born American management consultant, educator, and author, whose writings contributed to the philosophical and practical foundations of the modern business corporation. Source: Wikipedia.

[20] Our thanks to US missionary, John Heide, who blazed the trail ahead of us as the first AG US missionary focused on adults over fifty. He and his wife Judy, and others, encouraged us to move in this direction.

21 Dr. Chuck Stecker, A Chosen Generation, achosengeneration.info

22 NAE (National Association of Evangelicals), nae.net

23 NAE Conversion Statistics,
nae.net/when-americans-become-christians

24 Awana, awana.org

25 Gleanings for the Hungry, gleanings.org . YES! Gleanings Video:
youtube.com/watch?v=v1hw9-rOkCo

26 Who Stole my Church? What to Do When the Church You Love Tries
to Enter the 21st Century, Gordon MacDonald, published by Thomas
Nelson, 2010.

27 *Great is Thy Faithfulness* is a popular Christian hymn written
by Thomas Chisholm (1866–1960) with music composed by William
M. Runyan (1870–1957).

28 Cedar Valley Church, Bloomington, MN, cvchurch.org

29 John Piper quote is from a 2000 video, Don't Waste Your Life (Clip
from Passion OneDay 2000), youtube.com/watch?v=0sIqvQmT5IU.
John Piper is an American Calvinist Baptist pastor and author, founder
and leader of desiringGod.org, and chancellor of Bethlehem College &
Seminary in Minneapolis, Minnesota.

30 Sidney Aaron "Paddy" Chayefsky (1923 – 1981) was an American
playwright, screenwriter and novelist.

31 Joshua Becker is a former pastor and current speaker, blogger, and
minimalist who reminds others that "the best things in life aren't
things." becomingminimalist.com/about-us

[32] Celebrate Recovery is now in over 29,000 churches worldwide! A Christ-centered recovery program. celebraterecovery.com

[33] Don't be confused by the name; *Teen Challenge* is not just for teens. It's a Christ-centered, faith-based solution for youth, adults, and families struggling with life-controlling problems, such as addiction. teenchallengeusa.com

[34] *Dress a Girl Around the World* is a program of Hope 4 Women International, a nondenominational, independent Christian organization. dressagirlaroundtheworld.com

[35] Gideons International is an evangelical Christian association founded 1899 in Wisconsin . The Gideons' primary activity is distributing copies of the Bible free of charge. www2.gideons.org

[36] Prison Fellowship® trains and inspires churches and communities—inside and outside of prison—to support the restoration of those affected by incarceration. prisonfellowship.org

[37] Big Brother, Big Sister: bbbs.org

[38] Sam and Colleen Parsons have been touching lives in rest homes for years. goodnewsministry.net

[39] Meals on Wheels America: mealsonwheelsamerica.org

[40] Stephen Ministries is a not-for-profit Christian education organization founded in 1975 that produces training and resources known for their excellence, practicality, psychological integrity, and theological depth. These resources cover topics such as caring ministry, assertive relating, spiritual gifts discovery, grief support, spiritual growth, and more. stephenministries.org

[41] Royal Family Kids, making moments matter for foster children, rfk.org

[42] Samaritan's Purse Operation Christmas Child, samaritanspurse.org/what-we-do/operation-christmas-child/

[43] Cat's in the Cradle, youtube.com/watch?v=KUwjNBjqR-c

[44] Mount Hermon's year-round Christ-centered camps, conferences and concerts serve the entire family. mounthermon.org

[45] Barna Study, State of the Church 2016, barna.com/research/state-church-2016

[46] Let's not over-complicate this important invitation. Here is a simple *sinner's prayer* example: "*God, I know that I am a sinner. I know that I deserve the consequences of my sin. However, I am trusting in Jesus Christ as my Savior. I believe that His death and resurrection provided for my forgiveness. I trust in Jesus and Jesus alone as my personal Lord and Savior. Thank you Lord, for saving me and forgiving me! Amen!*" Source: gotquestions.org/sinners-prayer.html

[47] Generation to Generation, powered by Encore.org, the Gen2Gen campaign helps people over 50 find new ways to improve the lives of young people who need champions. generationtogeneration.org

[48] Allow me to recommend a very practical resource from fellow missionary, Jim Hall. *THRIVE - Discipler's Guide: Mentoring new Christians through One PLANTs One Discipleship (2012)*. amazon.com/dp/0615705561

[49] In January 2013, *ServeNow* was launched to serve people in need by caring for orphans, widows, underprivileged children and youth as well as equipping the Church for greater fulfillment of its ministry and providing humanitarian assistance where needed. weservenow.org

[50] Taylor-Johnson Temperament Analysis. A worthwhile personality assessment for individuals, couples, and families. tjta.com

[51] goodreads.com/quotes/390887 I'll add my brother-in-law Jeff Stone's response to this quote. "Well, it's obvious D.L. Moody wasn't a golfer!"

[52] War Room, Kendrick Brothers, 2015. Official trailer: youtube.com/watch?v=mll-XY9t_Lw

[53] E.B. White, goodreads.com/quotes/542655

[54] Do Hard Things, Alex and Brett Harris, 2008, therebelution.com/books/do-hard-things

[55] Prime Time: How Baby Boomers Will Revolutionize Retirement and Transform America, Marc Freedman, 2002, published by Public Affairs Press, pages 123-126, story highlighted on back cover.

[56] Google Christian RV ministries, and a plethora of opportunities appear. Some are denominationally affiliated, such as US MAPS-RV, usmaps.ag.org, and others like the SOWER (Servants On Wheels Ever Ready) Ministry are non-denominational, sowerministry.org

[57] Foster grandparenting, through AmeriCorps, nationalservice.gov/programs/senior-corps/senior-corps-programs/fostergrandparents

[58] Sticky Faith: Everyday Ideas to Build Lasting Faith in Your Kids, Dr. Kara E. Powell & Dr. Chap Clark, published by Zondervan, 2011. fulleryouthinstitute.org/stickyfaith

[59] Growing Young, Kara Powell, Jake Mulder, and Brad Griffin, Fuller Youth Institute, published by Baker Publishing Group, 2016. churchesgrowingyoung.com

[60] Asian American Christian Fellowship, aacf.org

[61] McLean Bible Church, impacting lives with the Gospel of Jesus Christ, beginning with the greater Washington, DC area. mcleanbible.org

[62] City Impact Adopt-a-Building, sfcityimpact.com/aab/

[63] Chasing God, chasinggod.com,

[64] My dad, Harold Wick, was an amazing man with a rough start in life, orphaned in Norway at the age of eight: yestoserve.org/yes-blogs/orphan-fear. In addition to building homes, he was a visionary lay leader for Life Center, a vibrant church in Tacoma, securing the property for that campus and serving as building chair twice for the church and also for Life Manor.

[65] A Lord-Built House, by Roger Lentz, beckenhorstpress.com/a-lord-built-house

[66] Not to be confused with *Ted Talks*, our Ted doesn't talk, but we like to talk about him. Produced by Jeremy Wick, 2010. yestoserve.org/ted

[67] The Villages, thevillages.com

[68] Live Oaks Community Church, liveoakschurch.org

[69] Psalm 23: 1-3a (NASB)

[70] An audio version of Erica sharing Joe Capri's story is available at yestoserve.org/yes-podcast/erica-capri

[71] This line jumped off the page for Joe Fuiten, one of my young-adult-years mentors, which he highlighted in a farewell sermon almost four decades ago, as he left his associate pastor role at Life Center, my home church in Tacoma.

[72] Seattle Pacific University, founded in 1891. "Engaging the culture, changing the world." spu.edu

[73] Surprised by Joy: The Shape of My Early Life, C.S. Lewis, published by A Harvest Book Harcourt, Inc., 1966.

[74] *Surprised by Joy,* Sonnet, William Woodsworth, poetryfoundation.org/poems/50285/surprised-by-joy

[75] "ELIC sends passionate, committed people to work in some of the most remarkable places on earth." elic.org

[76] Focus on the Family Online Mentoring is one example. focusonthefamily.com/promos/online-mentors

[77] Teaching to Change Lives: Seven Proven Ways to Make Your Teaching Come Alive, Dr. Howard Hendricks, Random House Digital Inc.

[78] Mission Builders International, the volunteer placement branch of Youth With A Mission, connecting Christians to frontline missions, missionbuilders.org

[79] Youth With A Mission (YWAM), ywam.org

[80] We'll end these notes with one final story. Several years ago Judy was en route to a YES! sewing party and was hit nearly head-on by another vehicle. Fortunately, there were no injuries, but our ministry vehicle, generously donated years earlier, was totaled.

We prayed for miraculous provision, and word circulated that YES! needed a compact SUV or sedan. Privately, we expressed our desires to the Lord: a compact SUV, 2000 or newer, with under 100,000 miles, and a miracle—not just a good deal. Our insurance loaner was about to expire on Friday, February 1.

On the preceding Sunday afternoon, our jaws dropped as we read an email from Lanette Henderson from Chico, California. "This may sound crazy, but the Lord told me to give you my compact SUV, a 2002 Ford Escape. It has 98,000 miles, and I can have it ready for you by this Friday, February 1."

What an incredible faith booster! Thank you, Jesus, for Lanette and others like her who listen and respond to Your voice, even at considerable personal cost and sacrifice. We're still gratefully driving that same vehicle, reminded of God's miraculous provision and the many people who help fuel this ministry.

Made in the USA
Columbia, SC
04 January 2018